Patrolling the Darkness

*How a City's First Female Police Officer
Loses Herself—And is Arrested by God*

By
Janell C. Armstrong

His Purpose Publishing
Omaha, Nebraska

Published by: His Purpose Publishing
                  Omaha, Nebraska

ISBN 13: 978-0692361467
ISBN 10: 0692361464
Library of Congress Control Number: 2015930145
Copyright © 2014 Janell C. Armstrong

First Printing May 2015

DEDICATION

I would like to dedicate this book to all members of law enforcement and their families.

And to my husband, Paul, I thank you gigantically for your ever-present support. Together we served God, raised yours, mine and our children, who, by the way, tolerated two personal police presences in their lives. Of course they would say they tolerated the entire city and county law enforcement personnel. In spite of occasional negatives, together we enjoyed our careers. Your care and concern has been a great uplifting element in my life.

Unless you've been there, you cannot fully appreciate the sacrifices these men and women make in their dedication to the job and their concern for the plight of others. Their families keep up a brave front, when in fact they live on pins and needles, hoping their loved ones will come home in one piece – without emotional baggage – either when the shift is over or later, depending upon the severity of the case they are working on.

A giant shout-out to a terrific friend, Linda Aldrich, who spent a great deal of her time editing this work. Thank you Linda, we still need to do lunch. And to my many encouragers along the way, I say Thank you.

I also want to thank a Great God, who watches over all who watch over His!

Watch I
Approximately 1990

FOREWORD

Initially, this book was written like a journal, as a method for healing in my life. I spent twenty-five years on the police department. I was the first female officer in the city, originally working in the Juvenile Division.

In the beginning my peers approached me with caution, then with apprehension, and eventually as a colleague. Many of the command addressed me with respect and appreciation for my accomplishments. However, a few treated me with disdain and even disgust. I have changed the names in this book—not to protect those few, but to save their friends, spouses, significant others and children from undue criticism and embarrassment.

I am grateful for the gracious true leaders, and even for the vicious ones. The Lord has used the experience to teach me forgiveness and to remind me of the mercy He has provided me.

TABLE OF CONTENTS

Patrolling the Darkness

How a City's First Female Police Officer
Loses Herself—And is Arrested by God

ONE

In the Beginning

Jeremiah 29:11—"For I know the plans I have for you," declares the LORD, "plans to prosper you and not to harm you, plans to give you hope and a future)..." (NIV)

I was an executive secretary to the most gracious, understanding, patient, generous man in the world. So what would possess me to pursue another career? I was stifled working inside an office building all day. The voice from the small box that sat on my desk kept calling my name. I always liked my name, until I had to answer to it so many times a day. I was shut up inside, from 8 A.M until 5 P.M. without the freedom to venture out, throw my head back and smell the fresh air.

Well, sometimes it didn't smell so fresh.

The largest industry for 100 years, in our fair city, was our stockyards and packing companies. Every now and then the odors drifted to the downtown area. Being confined to a cubicle was disturbing to the restless characteristic that was a major part of my personality.

Life was flowing very evenly for me in 1972. I had a job that kept my two small boys and I fairly secure. At least I was more comfortable than we had been in the past. We were able to have groceries in the house for an entire week. We could actually go buy fast food occasionally.

The company that I worked for was top notch and all of the people that I worked with were very good friends. However, I had this restless yearning inside me to get outside. So when a newspaper article was pointed out to me one morning, regarding a Police Matron retiring and that a Policewoman would replace her, I started to contemplate the possibility.

A close friend, who I am sure was weary of listening to me complain about my present career choice, strongly encouraged me to apply for this position. Truthfully, she just wanted me to quit complaining. And it worked.

I went to the City Personnel Office, picked up the paperwork and promptly filled it out and submitted it. The next month was a complete whirlwind; a written test, a physical exam, oral interview, and very shallow agility test. Six women survived the initial testing. By the time of the oral interviews, two women remained on the list. We were both in the area of 30 years of age, both divorced and both had children.

The panel interviewing us made it very clear that they were less than pleased with the fact that we were divorced. The panel voiced their opinion by explaining, that the department consisted of men (surprise, surprise) and that divorced women were a definite temptation. I was questioned at length in regard to the state of my health and particularly whether or not I had any problems with my back. It was mentioned that the physical exam showed some signs of calcium.

See Page 91

The very morning after my oral interview, I visited my family doctor and questioned him about the severity of calcium deposits and the complications they might present in the future. The doctor explained that it was quite normal for a person of my age to have some calcium deposits and that there was no possible way that they could affect my performance. He left me with the ever-popular statement, "Not to worry."

In spite of all the objections, I started my first day on the Border City Police Dept. on May 15, 1972. Thirty years of age and now I wondered if I had made the biggest mistake of my life. Too late now—I had a prestigious profession and a $54 a month increase in pay and good health insurance and what more could I ask?

Monday morning sixteen others and I started recruit training at the Police Academy. I was launched into weeks of learning the State Code, the Municipal Code, and report-writing techniques. While the men attended combat classes and hands on traffic training, I was sent to the Juvenile Division where I listened and learned about Youth Crime, Juvenile Laws, Human Services and the intricacies of the Juvenile Court. I was offered the opportunity to learn how to handle and shoot the Smith and Wesson, snub nose, .38 cal. revolver that was issued to me. For ten weeks, this was the procedure followed.

At the end of week two, I was called into the office of the training Lieutenant. It became apparent, right off the bat, that I was being interrogated. Now, having always been straight forward and prone to telling things the way they were, I just answered all of the questions asked very truthfully.

Lt.:	Where were you last night?
Myself:	At a local bar with a male friend.
Lt.:	What does your friend do for a living?
Myself:	He works for an agricultural based company?
Lt:	Did you know that he was a married man? And that his wife's name is Jennifer?
Myself:	Yes
Lt.:	Did you know that he has two children and that their names are Mark and Michelle?
Myself:	Yes
Lt.:	Did you know that he attends a Catholic Church in his hometown?
Myself:	Yes (I am thinking – and your point is?)
Lt.:	And what time did you leave this bar?
Myself:	Around 1 A.M.
Lt.:	And where did you go when you left there?
Myself:	I am starting to get the idea that he already knew where we went and so I said that we went to breakfast. (Actually we went back to his hotel room)
Lt.:	You are lying!

Myself: You're right, but I don't get the purpose for this little conversation. What has my personal life to do with my employment?

At this point, I really wished I had not asked this question as I was told in the most abusive manner why it was the department's business what I did and where I did it, and who I did it with. I was told that for one year I was on probation and that they need not have any cause for terminating my employment should they see that I was becoming a source of embarrassment to them.

I want to add here that I was well acquainted with a number of seasoned police officers and I was furrowing my brow at this point as I was well aware of the behavior of some of the already certified police officers and they were considered top notch.

The Lieutenant's reprimand continued with the warning that bars were not an appropriate place for a Police Officer and that it would not be tolerated. It also would not be tolerated if I should continue to "see" a married man. (I thought, *Wow—I am in real trouble here*, as I totally restricted myself to married men. This way, I didn't have to worry about making or accepting commitments.) Past hurts had distorted my thinking considerably, but at the time, I thought this was perfectly normal thinking.

I then brazenly inquired as to whether or not the department was monitoring my activities after I left the building. Another error in judgment on my part, as I was told, "That is none of your damn business. Just behave yourself in a respectable manner and you'll have nothing to fear."

I took his response as a "Yes."

I left that office at the end of the day in a complete state of "Who cares?"

Well, certainly I did. I could not lose this job. I had two young boys ages 8 and 10 to support, and I tended to get a little hungry myself once in a while. But the emotion that I experienced most was fear: the fear of completely not understanding their motives and the fear that accompanied the knowledge that my privacy had been completely violated. I was not moral enough, at that point in my life, to be embarrassed about being confronted about a relationship with a married man. I certainly was fearful that someone had watched my every move from the previous evening while I had been completely unaware of his or her presence.

I shared this fiasco of an interview with my Captain and he gave me the 5-minute version of how the department worked and that they really didn't want to hire a female, but due to a federal grant they were forced to do so. In other words, I was not a very popular addition according to the administration.

My Captain's advice: "Keep your nose clean for twelve months and then it takes a pretty big situation to separate you from your job."

Gee—now I felt better. I went home, called my male friend and discouraged him from continuing the relationship, at least for the next year.

I might as well tell you that he didn't wait around or check on me from time to time. He just checked out of my life. Meaningful relationship, wouldn't you say?

The weeks moved on and so did the surveillance. I was not being introduced to the guys who secretly kept me company, but I recognized them as men who worked in the same building.

I would think to myself, *These sleuths are not good at this, unless they don't care that I'm aware that they are constantly with me.*

I lived in a large apartment complex and during the evenings a nameless Captain would spend night after night in the parking lot. Initially I assumed he was spying on a drug ring or something adventurous. But when his car left the lot when mine did, I knew I had that figured inaccurately.

I'd like to be able to report that I instantly turned into a respectable, meek, compliant recruit, but I didn't. I still led the same life with the exception of the bars. I figured they were off my social calendar for the year.

So I invited my friends to my house to play cards and other indoor games. We weren't the rowdiest group in the neighborhood, but we weren't the most boring, either.

I moved from the apartment complex to a small house in a secluded, off-the-street area. I thought this would be more difficult to watch and I also wanted to get my boys away from all the corrupt influences that could be found in multiple dwelling units. Their worst influence probably lived in the house, but then as yet I was unaware.

I hadn't been living in the house three weeks when I noticed lights in the upstairs of a house, directly half a block to the south of mine. The house had been vacant since I moved in. By this time I had become an itty-bit paranoid and so I naturally imagined that the light, which was not constant, belonged to a policeman's flashlight. How in the world could I know for sure? Was someone watching my every move even at 11:00 at night? Would this ever end? And once again, have I made the biggest mistake of my life?

I had to know if I was being imaginative or if my assessments were accurate. I left my house by the back door, walked to the alley and headed south. At the end of the alley, parked directly behind the vacant house, was a green Dodge. The Dodge was used as an undercover car and was parked every day in the basement of the police station. My suspicions were confirmed.

I strolled back to my house, looked for some poster paper, and wrote a note in very large letters: YOU CAN GO BACK TO WORK NOW, I AM GOING TO BED, and taped it to the front door of my house where it could easily be read through binoculars from the previously vacant house.

For the next six weeks, I saw the green Dodge a lot, both night and day. I would see the "disguised" police car in the area with a lone driver, or it would be three cars behind me.

By this time I was feeling very violated. Today the average citizen, caught doing this, would be charged with stalking. Now I know, God had a plan. Little did I know at the time that I was going to be a part of it.

TWO

May I Put Away the Books?

Proverbs 9:9—Instruct a wise man and he will be wiser still; teach a righteous man and he will add to his learning. (NIV)

Miraculously, I finished the recruit-training phase of my probation year. I could put away the law books and get into the practical side of juvenile investigations.

See Pages 92 – 93

What a relief to be working for a Captain who at least left the appearance of caring about me as a person. At this point, I wasn't even concerned if his attitude was sincere. I just relished the fact that I did not feel completely scrutinized.

The first two weeks were spent becoming adapted to the new surroundings. The end of my first day in Juvenile, Captain Jay asked if I would give him a ride to the car dealership that was working on his vehicle. I agreed to do so. I did fear that my "protectors" would misinterpret the Captain's presence in my car but he was the Captain.

We walked to my car, which was parked, on a side street about a block from the station. I opened the unlocked door, got into the driver's seat, took the key from above the visor and started the car. I obeyed all the traffic laws while transporting him to his destination.

The following day, I came to my desk and the Captain gave me the normal runaway reports to study. Standard Operating memos were required to be read and then filed appropriately. After all required work was accomplished, Captain Jay gave me the new daily log from the night before and asked if I would circle all the stolen vehicle reports. This log contained all the police calls for the past 24 hours. I did so and returned it to him. He showed me where it was kept and then asked that I make that a daily routine.

For several weeks I circled the stolen vehicle reports and placed the logs in the proper place. I finally asked the Captain why I had to circle just the stolen vehicle reports. He said, "Just keep doing it, one day you will see."

I continued, but with every entry I circled I thought, "This is really a waste of time."

A few days passed and I asked again, "Why am I doing this?" His response, "You're doing a good job, you'll see one day."

After my shift that day, I headed to my car, opened the unlocked door, got the key from above the visor and started the engine. Just that swiftly, I GOT IT.

The following morning I said to the Captain, "Do I need to circle these reports anymore? I am not leaving my car door unlocked or the key in the vehicle any longer." He retorted, "I knew you would get it sooner or later."

At this time, I was living in a part of town that was considered somewhat rough. I still had no intentions of leaving the area as this was what I could afford and it was close to the day care. An abrupt change occurred in my thinking when my 10-year-old son came home and reported that a kid in his class pulled a knife on him at school that day. I immediately started looking for affordable housing in another area.

At the very same time, many were encouraging me, including a very insistent Mother, that I consider enrolling my children in parochial school. Mother's theories included the fact that all children should have a Christian Foundation. She emphatically reminded me that I had this opportunity and it should be afforded to my children. At this point, I thought (but did not say), What good had my "Christian education" done for me?

At that point in my life she was so ashamed of me that when I agreed to enroll my children in the parochial school in which she taught, she asked me not to reveal to anyone that I was her daughter. I was crushed and hurt, yet I did understand her humiliation. I was the first in her family to ever divorce. I made no attempt to hide my lifestyle. My mother showed me love and affection in private, but was very reserved with me in public.

»

My mother and another teacher, Sister Grace, taught the 4th grade. So, of course, when my boys approached the 4th grade, Sister Grace was their teacher. The Catholic nuns were not foreign to me. I had attended Catholic School from 7th grade forward. Sister Grace was a very unusual teacher. She was different from any I had ever encountered before. I had a very high reverence for the men and women who had devoted their lives to "the church." I want you to notice that I said "the church," as I really didn't believe, at this point, that anyone dedicated their lives to "a Lord."

I was soon to discover the difference. It became apparent to me immediately that Sister Grace was a non-judgmental person who really took an interest in my boys. She sincerely cared about their education and their home. Sister Grace started making occasional visits to my home. At first she said she liked to visit all of her student's homes. I thought that was reasonable. However, she started visiting ours quite often. I could never pinpoint when she might drop by, so I couldn't very well prepare for her visits.

Many times she would venture into my house while my friends were present. We might be playing poker, or we might be drinking, or we might have been drinking all afternoon. Sister Grace was always loving, kind, compassionate, and would not gasp, shrink back in horror or politely excuse herself. At times, she just joined in the laughter and was supportive and appeared approving.

We became very good friends. Whenever I needed childcare for a legitimate purpose, Sister Grace offered to be there for the boys. Legitimate purposes included doctor's appointments, grocery shopping, police related meetings or school activities. Trips to the bars or the racetrack did not apply. On occasion I would be called in to search female prisoners. Some of these occurrences happened in the middle of the night. At these times she would come to my house and stay with the boys until I returned, even if she had to sneak out of the convent.

Needless to say Sister Grace became a very best friend that lived in a completely different world. Never, ever did Sister Grace lecture or preach to me about my "colorful lifestyle" or the effect that it might be having on my boys. Never, ever did she make light of my vibrant friendships or the man that was sharing my home. Her immediate friends told her that I was hopeless as a candidate for the Kingdom of God. She just kept being my friend and encouraged me to get the boys involved in church.

During this same time I was learning how the juvenile system functioned.

Shortly after being assigned in Juvenile, another officer and I received a case involving a 9-month-old baby who was hospitalized, in a coma, and the possibility of recovery was very slim. My limited experience left me with the attitude that this case should not be very difficult to investigate. How many people could possibly have had contact with this child? The child had been taken by ambulance to the hospital from the babysitter's residence. The babysitter was a licensed childcare worker. She claimed that after the baby was left at her home, the baby was placed on a bed and did not wake up.

When an attempt was made to wake her, by mid-morning, there was no response and she was turning blue. The investigation turned toward the father, who was already considered abusive and very strange. The facts proved that the father had not been with the child since the previous day. The mother had taken the baby to childcare. Thus, our next interview

13

was with the mother. She was a teacher in a public school and so naturally we considered her to be a stable, well-adjusted person.

Yikes! About 10 minutes into the interview, she announced that she was a witch and that she was the leader of a coven of approximately 15 witches in the area. She proclaimed this just as readily as we might claim to be a Republican or a Democrat.

Imagine my stunned face. I had never encountered even the idea of such a chain of events. This was like outer space to me. Although she claimed that she had not mistreated her baby in any way, shape or form, she was one of the few people who was last with this child.

After interviews with the childcare worker, it was revealed to us that she had been reported before, for a similar incident. In the prior case, a few years before this, a child had been taken to the hospital from her home. After numerous sessions of questioning many different people, it was never determined who was responsible for this child's injuries. The 9-month-old baby girl died at the hospital after 9 weeks.

Now, we were asked to interview the mother's parents in regard to placement of a 2-year-old child from the same home. I was relieved to hear that the grandparents were anxious to be involved. My thought process resembled relief, as I knew the past generation was likely to be more responsible. The grandparents came to the Youth Bureau for the interview and after introductions, I started questioning. In an instant, I could not help but notice that the grandfather had on a bolo tie with the clasp being the shape of a serpent.

Now, I would not have been alarmed about this except that on his hand he had a ring that was also in the shape of a serpent. After the daughter had informed us of her connection with witchcraft, I did indeed become alarmed, as I knew the symbolism. Nothing to do but make up a detailed report and leave the decisions up to the Department of Human Services.

Education by experience is a lasting, learning event. I will never forget my introduction to the occult. I would run across it often in later years.

The books had been put away from my recruit-training phase but I would never cease referencing "the books" for answers to many questions along the way. And I thought the education period was over!!

God had a plan and I didn't have a clue.

THREE

Career- To Be or Not To Be

Psalm 142:3—When my spirit grows faint within me, it is you who know my way. In the path where I walk men have hidden a snare for me. (NIV)

In 1972 the words sexual discrimination meant nothing to me. I could not relate to a situation that might even indicate that such an incident had taken place. This phenomenon was so commonplace that it seemed only natural to me. I had been both a participant and the recipient of this type of behavior in the other realms of my life so it was a very unimportant element.

I did begin to notice situations in which I felt significantly less than comfortable. Not that I couldn't handle myself, of course. I was tough emotionally, physically and constitutionally and remarks could not possibly cause me any malice. It could, however, evoke emotions ranging from doubled-over pain of hurt to being covered with emotional grime and dirt that was not removable. So here I am, a hunk of flesh so covered with silt that the use of abrasives is already doomed and I am so anguished that I feel that I need to be surrounded by a steel spider's web, to be protected. Yet, I want to continue to fight and claw to hang on to this abusive job.

So I thought, in the first months of my newfound career. When introduced to one of my first trainers, his comment was, "I'll work with her, let's go out and investigate on the gravel roads."

The first few months, I was propositioned on a daily basis, not only by officers and command but also by FBI agents, attorneys, judges, clerks, and anyone else who might enter or pass by the building. I'm being a little facetious but that was the picture that I was seeing at the time. I made a firm decision from the start, right or wrong I would not make waves. I needed the job to support my boys and I wanted the acceptance of my peers.

Of course, the acceptance of my peers was somewhere in Outer Mongolia or beyond because it was nowhere in sight. On one occasion an officer that had been on the department a few years was being transferred to the Youth Bureau. On his first day, I saw him come into the division and proceed to the Captain's office. The Captain informed him that he would be working with me until he learned the procedures and then he would be on his own.

This fine officer announced to his new Captain in a voice that could not help but be overheard by all, including me: "I will not work with that woman."

Consequently, he was placed with me for much longer than any other new officer to the division.

Slowly, we became respectful of one another. I learned, much to my dismay, that I was picking up some important techniques from him and he learned a few very crucial elements of juvenile investigation from me. Keep in mind that we were forced to spend much time together as the Captain was going to make certain that he was learning to tolerate "that woman."

In the course of traveling in the same squad car day after day, it became known that I was a Catholic and that he indeed was a proud Protestant. So, in order to keep things from becoming boring, we started keeping track of the religious preferences of the recipients of juvenile records. Keeping a straight face, while filling in the blanks was often an impossible task.

A few months proved to be the factor that put us in the "best friend" category for the rest of our careers. We gained a common respect for each other professionally and religiously.

The first couple of months, I really questioned my decision in regard to taking the policewoman position. I saw circumstances in people's lives that disturbed me greatly. I had no idea that children were treated so badly or so neglected. I could not believe the standard that the department had set for me and not for the rest of the officers. I could not believe the continued scrutiny of my life and the horrid feeling it left in the pit of my stomach. I realized for the first time that the freedoms we so often take for granted are vitally important. I also was sharp enough to realize that mine were being abused.

After six months though, I started to feel the accomplishment of an investigation well done. I learned the gratitude of a parent when a youthful offender was treated with respect and still got the point of his criminal behavior. I felt appreciated by my immediate supervisors when an element of an investigation was accomplished due to my efforts. Put in very simple terms, I really was feeling that I'd found my niche.

Now, for the purpose of this written account, I have been on the department for eleven months. A memo from the Chief's office advised me that I needed to go to the city physician and have another back x-ray. He indicated there were some possible calcium deposits that showed up on my initial film and that these might create some problems for me down the road.

I immediately thought "Down what road?" I am thinking that I am not on a road but a giant slide, leading me right out of a police career. I did concur with the order and had additional x-rays taken.

For my own peace of mind, I went to my own physician and asked if calcium deposits found on an x-ray could possibly change drastically in a one-year period of time. My doctor consoled me with the fact that this would be highly unlikely. He also informed me again that it would be unusual if anyone my age did not have some calcium build up. I left his office possessing my normal state of confidence.

A month later that assurance came crashing into the pavement. The Police Chief met me on a street corner as I was returning from lunch. He announced that I should be out looking for another job, as my x-rays were very bad and that it appeared as though I would be disabled in ten years or so. He said this department could not keep me on. "You have two weeks and then you are done."

See Pages 94 – 95

I returned to my office feeling as though I had been hit with a wrecking ball. What could I do? Where would I go? What about my boys? How could this happen? What should I do next? Did I have any recourse? Could I trust anyone? Could I talk to anyone? Does anyone really want me here? Do I dare mention this in the Youth Bureau?

I had heard my fellow officers speak of an attorney that our Police Association used for their negotiations, etc. I contacted him and gave him a brief synopsis of the Chief's conversation, which had been short so it was very easy to remember. The lawyer told me to go to the Chief's office to see if he would give me a written summary of the physical situation. I was also to ask if there were other factors which entered into the decision to terminate my career. The Chief not only summarized the physical, but also gave me the whole detailed analysis in writing from the city doctor. He informed me this was the only set of circumstances *they* were concerned with.

After gaining the information that I had gone for, I dialed my attorney's office and he told me that he would "get to work on it." He adamantly suggested that I pack up some things and leave town for the weekend. Of course, I knew that he was tuggin' my toe so I told him that I didn't have anywhere to go or the funds to carry out a trip to nowhere. He simply reiterated that it would be in my best interest to leave town simply for the weekend and that on Monday I should return to work and continue to work as though my conversation with the Chief had not occurred.

Since I could not think of a wholesome and affordable family outing, I opted to leave my boys with their Grandmother and go to the horse races. Sounded like fun to me and of course I reasoned that I could use a little "fun" during this trying time. There is nothing more invigorating than standing at the fence and hollering, "Go you old plug, go! You know I couldn't afford that $2 I just plunked on your nose, now come on—hit the finish line first."

He didn't win and I didn't feel like I was having "fun" either. Inner turmoil, I surmised, is not a good ingredient to induce fun. Therefore, the weekend was long and I was anxious to pick up my boys and head for home.

Monday morning left me feeling as though I had a one-ton weight wrapped around my waist. I didn't want to get out of bed nor did I want to haul myself the three miles to the police station. What would I do if they sent me home? How could I handle the humiliation that I might feel with the eyes of 102 officers looking at me?

When I got past the humiliation and feeling of defeat, I was overcome with anger and a lot of anger. In one short weekend, I had yielded to every form of anger and rage that I knew existed and then I stooped to bitterness and a truck load of resentment for the faction(s) that were playing God (whoever that was) with my life.

I sat at the kitchen table and poured a cup of coffee while the boys ate their morning breakfast. I opened the front door, picked up the newspaper and carried it to the kitchen. I placed it under the Saturday and Sunday papers that I had missed over the weekend. I positioned them in chronological order to the left of my cup and saucer. I ushered the guys out the back door for their three-block trek to school. Gee, I hoped they would go straight to school.

What a relief, now I could relax for ten minutes before today's lengthy trip to the station. My first look at the paper produced a gasp of enormous proportion. My picture was strategically placed on the front page of the Saturday paper. "Policewoman Would Sue to Keep Her Job"—that was the headline. The article wasn't lengthy but ended in the statement that I was unable to be reached for comment. The picture was now clear as to why I was encouraged to leave the city for the weekend.

See Page 100

The complete reading of the newspapers was lost to racing thoughts that now bounced around in my head cavity. Oh, how in the world could I enter the police station after reading this article? My peers were not exactly ecstatic about my presence there anyway. Would I be ostracized upon entering the building? I didn't feel as though I had done anything wrong but I felt totally devalued. I reasoned that I might be more comfortable being cast into the lion's den.

All surprises have an element of shock whether good or bad. The amazement that I experienced upon my entry into the Police Department was overwhelming. The men that I worked with were extremely compassionate. I didn't believe that they were accepting of me as a police officer but I had no doubt that they acknowledged me as a person of value. What ease they brought to my return to employment after having been told that I was virtually done. New hope had been instilled in me.

Before the day was over, the City's Police Association had called a special meeting to discuss their attitude and stance in regard to the elements surrounding the Chief's announcement to me. The next day the meeting took place at 2 PM. At that time in police history, a new officer was not sworn into the association until their one-year probation period was over. I was one month away from that time span.

The Association voted overwhelmingly to support me in an effort to keep my job. I was amazed, and found that I had the ability to feel humbled. To this point, I thought rage, anger, hurt; degradation and doom were the only feelings that were able to pulse through my defeated being, now the new and monumental emotion of humility. The Association that was representative of the whole police department had now affirmed me.

Captain Ferrell, who represented a powerful force, within the department attended and made numerous attempts to intimidate members to vote against supporting me. His argument was that this action would be setting a precedent for all future recruits that were within their first year of employment. The many officers related that not supporting me would also set a precedent. Recruits could be released without any viable reason. The Captain eventually left the meeting in a huff after he realized that his viewpoint was not shared.

The whole political map of the department was still unknown to me at this time. I would later realize the tremendous limb that those officers walked out on when they backed a "female officer."

According to the Association's attorney, we had just won round one. I was asked to pick up my x-rays from the city doctor's office and deliver them to an Orthopedic Specialist. I called to make the appointment and was told that I would have to be referred by my family physician. I stopped at his office, related the current turn of events and he called an Orthopedic Specialist friend making an appointment there. The purpose was to have the specialist review the x-rays and to write an opinion in regard to the degree of disability that I could expect and when I could anticipate the onset.

Upon arriving at the specialist's office, I introduced myself to the receptionist and related the time of my appointment. She promptly informed me that I did not have an appointment. Funny, my calendar indicated that I had an appointment but then I had been known to lose keys, forget to pick up kids, send birthday cards three months late, or not send them at all. So, I might have gotten the date wrong. I asked the receptionist to look for another day in the week. She responded by saying that a Sergeant had picked up my x-rays and returned them to the city doctor's office after the Chief had called and cancelled my appointment.

The round of emotions started all over again, extreme anger, deep-seated resentment and a rage that I just did not feel would subside. My wildest imagination could not encompass the nerve of anyone who would cancel another's doctor appointment. I could not possibly fight the power of a structure such as the City Police and a doctor who represented the entire city.

I called my attorney again. He must be getting sick and tired of me. Well at least he recognized my voice by now. His advice was to make another appointment, retrieve, and deliver the x-rays to the same specialist. He would make the appointment himself. *Voilà*—the appointment was still intact and the doctor would see me now.

What a reception I received from this high-positioned professional. I had always held skilled, masterful people in the highest esteem, as I had been taught. This well-thought-of doctor was deliberately and excessively rude to me. He was abrasive in his tone and his examination was even more abusive. He talked with me as though I were a prostitute attempting to extort money from him.

I was beyond shock as both my attorney and my family doctor had told me what an exemplary person he was as well as a dedicated family man. I reminded myself that I would never want to be involved with such an "unblemished man." I could not even define him as a man. I immediately dubbed him a weasel.

Then, to add insult to my already injured existence, when I delivered the paperwork to the cashier prior to leaving the office I was presented with an enormous bill that did not at all coincide with the services provided. Anger again surfaced and I marched right back to the doctor's office and questioned his billing practices. His explanation was that he was anticipating litigation and thus the higher fee. He also spit the fact out that doctors did not like getting involved in lawsuits.

A few days passed and I received the letter I was expecting from my "specialist friend." Just as I suspected, the report indicated that I was normal in every way, at least as far as he could see. I couldn't wait to get this all-important letter to my attorney. Skeptical as I was, however, I made 10 copies before giving my only one away. This letter was sent to the Chief of Police who didn't acknowledge it. He never made an attempt to contact me about its content, nor did he answer any calls from my attorney.

See Pages 96 – 101

I simply just kept going to work. My confidence level was shaken but I dug myself out of the hole in which I felt buried, determined to put my best foot forward and thrive in this career I had chosen. I would not forget but I would go on.

My personal evaluation of this experience was that in spite of all the controversy, I was not living in a hostile atmosphere. I intended to go upward and onward in the Juvenile position and mind my p's and q's in order to have security for my boys and myself.

I was again pleasantly surprised when my Captain took me under his wing, advised me against harboring bitter feelings and to start a process of forgiveness. I admit that I was not prepared to do that as I had chosen to wallow in the muck rather than to rise above it. Instead of being judged, I was met with prayer and guidance and I don't mind telling you that I didn't relish either. There were cracks in the armor, however. God had a plan and believe me I didn't think I needed to be a part of it.

FOUR

Who in the World Am I?

Jeremiah 33:3—Call to me and I will answer you and tell you great and unsearchable things you do not know. (NIV)

Where am I? Not physically, I have not gone totally insane. I know my address. I know where I go to work. I am unsure though where I am emotionally. That tough woman that started this position is quite unaware of her inner being and where she is, let alone where she might want to be. Why *am* I here? Is there any rhyme or reason to my life? Is this *really* what I want to do with the rest of my life?

All of the sudden, I was overcome with questions about the direction of my life. Up until this point, I had just flitted along without any thought of a final destination. All at once I had an inclination to evaluate. The question of the hour remained. What in the world was I evaluating?

If the above sounds like total confusion to you—how do you think I felt? All these thoughts, emotions and feelings were running around in my head with no direction.

While all of this was going on in my mind, I was still drinking, but with reserve. The bars were a place of socializing for me. They also provided an escape from the buzzing in my head.

I also was nurturing a long relationship with a married man. Because I could not refer to him by name a lot of the time, my friends and I just called him George. (This was one of those off again on again associations. More off than on.)

My rationalization went like this. He did not live at home. They were separated. (No attempt to divorce but then who wanted a permanent relationship anyway.) In this scenario, I did not have to make any commitment and I definitely didn't have to expect one. He was totally unavailable both emotionally and from a marital point of view. I did sincerely care about him and convinced myself that the feeling was mutual. I, at least, did not have to go out and look for another meaningful relationship, if that concept even existed. We had fun together and totally disregarded the element called long-term.

Not only had I been evaluating my own inner being but I also began to appraise the life that I was providing for my boys. They now were ages 10 and 12. I began to see that there were more elements necessary to raise fruitful children than the mere outward care of their daily physical needs. Where does one start to fulfill such enormous responsibilities? I guess that I will need to sleep on that one. I don't even know where to start. Up until now I had just simply taken one day at a time trying to keep my head above water while having as much fun as possible. I did make a firm resolve to determine what direction was needed in my life to accomplish all these thoughts running around in my head.

All of these things were swimming around in my cranium and at the same time I could not even imagine how I could abandon the form of life that I now believed I was content with.

While I was contemplating all of this I was also celebrating my 32nd birthday. George had left my house about three days earlier after removing items that he had given me. My understanding was that we were through. George and I had been squabbling about who knows what. He was never consistent about his whereabouts. I could not count on him being with me on any given day. I didn't care that he wasn't with me all the time but at least if I could plan for the times when he was there. And of course there was always the ongoing accusation that he was (and he was) seeing someone else.

How delighted I was when he showed up at my house with a birthday cake all wrapped with a pretty bow. Maybe I could find myself and combine that newfound individual with a genuine sincere relationship with George. He obviously did care for me. Why else would he bring me a birthday cake after the horrible things that we said to each other? I made a pot of coffee to go with the cake and hoped that we could sit down and discuss the episodes we have had in the past and try to recapture our profound desire for each other.

The coffee is poured and I untie the ribbon on the boxed cake. I had received so many nice gifts from George but I am feeling that a birthday cake is even more special as it is so personal.

I opened the cake and the printing says Happy Birthday Bitch.

The mood of the special occasion immediately turned to chaos. My voice could have been heard at the border of the nearest state. It was telling Mr. Nice guy that he should get out and take whatever he wanted as he was not welcome in my house again.

He made his grand exit, as I was throwing the precious cake at him. He slammed the front door. All of the paint that I had just applied to the doorframe cracked and peeled, adding insult to the already burning injury. Now I not only had cake all over my living room floor but I had cracked paint mingled in the chocolate frosting. Not very wise of me to throw the cake. Chocolate is my very favorite and it was hardly edible now.

As I appraised the damage to my current paint job, the phone rang. It was Sister Grace just checking on me. I was very well composed until she started to inquire about me and then I broke down and started to cry. Why in the world was all of this happening to me? What had I done to deserve such continued treatment? Grace was, as always, non-judgmental and very concerned. I shared with her the scene that had just taken place at my house.

For two years now Grace had been sitting back and observing and being very supportive. On this occasion, although she was reassuring, she was also offering advice. She listened very quietly and then asked me if I had ever prayed about the direction of my life and about my ongoing relationship with George.

I told her that I definitely prayed about my life. Then she had the audacity to ask me to repeat to her the words that I prayed. Well I replied with the statement, "I think that my prayer life (or lack of it) is very personal and I don't need to share it with anyone."

So there! Very calmly she said that the way we pray is very important. She indicated that it was utterly mandatory that we pray unselfishly and with proper motives.

Very reluctantly I told Grace that I simply asked the Lord to help the boys and me to have a better life and that I prayed that George and I would finish this drastic relationship once and for all.

She responded by telling me that in order to pray effectively, I needed to admit that I needed God and that I wanted to have a personal friendship and relationship with him.

My thought process immediately went to, "Well how in the world do you accomplish that?"

Just as though I actually voiced that question, Grace responded, "Just acknowledge that your life to this point has been one of sin and ask God to forgive you." (Acknowledging the state of my life was a no brainer.) She then told me that Jesus would have hung on the cross just for me, even if I had been the only person on earth. She further advised me to ask him to come in and take control of my life. She said I should be praying for

George. I thought that just a little odd but hey, I could give it a try.

After completing our conversation, I immediately took the time to pray in the same vein that Grace had suggested. I had never simply talked with a Lord that I couldn't see as though I were talking with another person in my room. I had learned to say only written prepared prayers and it was very, very awkward to speak with a God that I had only known by way of prayer books and teachings.

I asked this invisible God to help me to prepare a more acceptable life for myself, and my boys. I asked Him to provide happiness and contentment for George so that we would not be tempted to reconnect. I asked Him to guide me in my everyday decisions and I asked Him to possibly provide a stable male companion in my life for both myself and for my children. I added that it would be a bonus if I could love this man and if he could love me. (In my limited thinking, this was nigh on near to impossible.)

I went to bed and slept with such a peace. I had never before experienced this form of peace. I really did not dwell on or worry about the words of that prayer being fulfilled because to be very truthful, I did not expect it. I simply expected the days to proceed and eventually events in my life would replay themselves all over again.

I never again heard from George. I began to see life from a different perspective. I started to become interested in me, inside and out. Instead of planning fantasy scenarios, my attention became more focused on my boys.

Maybe Captain Jay had an inkling of an idea of what it took to begin to establish a "better life." For two years he had been attempting to introduce me to a life that was more complete. His method, of course, was to increase my awareness of "issues of faith." Each morning, Captain Jay and a few of our colleagues would meet in lieu of coffee and they would spend that time praying. After numerous attempts, and to appease my Commanding Officer, I agreed to join them, although I knew that this was one of those kooky, flaky, hypercritical, super spiritual groups that devoured and used mind control on people.

My first impression of the "prayer meeting" group was not that at all. These were people, not unlike myself who just worked every day and who had the same struggles in life as I. What a surprise when I found that I was mistaken *again*.

Reluctantly I became an observer, attempting to be a part without actually participating, a little like watching a basketball game but not really caring which team won the game. Initially, I could listen to the ease with which these sincere people (even if a little odd) could talk to the Lord as though He were right in the center of our circle of participants.

As much as I resisted the concept that this whole process had any worth or meaning, I was continually drawn back to being an observer of the sessions. One by one, I started to notice that prayers that were spoken within this group were being answered. I was just a little more than astonished. Most of the answers appeared to be small things. Doctor's reports being positive, car keys being found, investigations successfully completed, and arrests being made without negative incidents. However, there were some answers that seemed to defy the core of my belief system (if I really did possess such a thing.)

Prayers were delivered to the Lord in regard to healing of family members who appeared to have no hope of survival and *whammo!*—a couple of days later reports of advancements in health conditions were received which offered hope and other days communications were received indicating complete and total healing. Now the ability to disbelieve was becoming more difficult.

Oh well, what could it hurt to allow the wall, that kept people and especially the Lord (or so I thought) a good distance away from me, to come down for a very short, maybe a minute period of time?

I even inched into the "group" enough to mention concerns that I had that might be mentioned in prayer. Of course I couldn't voice them myself, as I did not feel adequate of speech. But even more than the lack of eloquence of verbal delivery, I felt that I lacked the relationship that I would expect of someone asking me to do them a favor. I operated out of a feeble mental capacity. Therefore, I could not understand a God that accepted me and my prayers in spite of all my imperfections.

Now I am accepting some ownership of "our group." It started with three people, then five, and then eight and within the lifespan went to thirteen. Coffee breaks had never been so peaceful. For as long as I live, I will always be in awe of prayers answered. One of the major miracles that I witnessed was my own conformation and eventual willingness to accept and develop a relationship with Jesus.

The second giant miracle I became a part of involved a fellow worker.

Adam worked out of the same division as I and was very outspoken about the fact that he believed that our "group" was very "wrong" for meeting in a public government building for the purpose of praying. In order to correct this travesty, he went to the Chief of Police who had granted us the permission and time slot in the first place. When that did not produce results, he went to the City Manager who explained to Adam that we all were allowed to spend our coffee breaks in any way that we chose.

Now Adam was an eager beaver and when he clamped his teeth onto this large tree he refused to let go. His next step was to approach the City Council. He was shot down at that level also, which left him very antagonistic to the individuals who participated in the "group." It was difficult for him to retaliate in conversation or deed to the leader of this "group" as he happened to be Adam's Captain but it was very easy to badger me as I was not only junior in seniority but I was also a "woman."

Adam worked daily at antagonizing me. Since this serene life was new to me, I did not accept the persecution very well. My thought processes always told me that I must, beyond all costs, defend myself, and my position. So, I tried to prove to Adam that my newfound belief was justified by Scripture, of which I knew very little.

Although we worked individually in cars, occasionally Captain Jay would request that I help Adam to get caught up, which would require us to work out of the same car. Here I thought that Captain Jay liked me. Instead of allowing me to have peaceful days, I now had to spend horrendous days with Adam as he tormented me in an attempt to deprogram my changing thought processes.

Slowly I attempted to be the loving—no matter what—person that I thought Jesus would want me to be. I tried to answer Adam's derogatory remarks with a Spirit of Love and no matter how negative he became, I attempted to guide him to a positive stance.

Eventually, he started to share his life and his viewpoint with me in a concerned way. He had a 6-year-old daughter with extreme kidney problems who was not going to live unless she received a donor kidney. His marriage was faltering under the weight of all of the strain and everything appeared hopeless. He had always considered himself an agnostic and could not make sense of anyone who relied on anything except his or her own resources.

Adam did not ask me to provide this information to others so I simply informed him that I would pray for him and his daughter. Some time later he informed me that Beth was scheduled for surgery for a new kidney.

I asked Adam if I could go see her before her surgery. I visited her a few times before the actual surgery and I talked with her at great length about Jesus who loved her and wanted to go into surgery with her to hold her hand. We instantly became good friends and she was the bravest, most courageous 6-year-old I had ever seen.

The morning of the surgery, I accompanied Adam to the hospital and saw Beth before she was wheeled into the "room of miracles." Beth asked me to say a prayer for her, which I did—right in front of her Dad—and then she said to him, "Daddy, if something happens I will see you on the other side. I will be with Jesus."

I had never talked with her about "the other side" and we were both astounded. God honored our prayer and Beth recovered and did very well after her transplant. When she recovered sufficiently, I occasionally asked if I could take her to church and Sunday school. Permission granted, and she grew quickly and strongly in the Lord.

One day Adam said to me, "Jane, how can you remain friendly toward me when you know how diligently I have worked to break up your little 'prayer group'?"

Straight from the Holy Spirit's mouth (as my inclination was to harshly and adamantly reprimand him for his rotten attitude) to Adam's ears I heard my voice explain, "It's difficult to understand when you don't have all the facts. I have known all along that God was pleased with our group. The Word says, 'Wherever two or three are gathered in my name, there I will be in the midst of them.' But I also know that God's purposes and our prayers could be fulfilled with or without the group. For instance, I have been praying during the entire time that we have been working together out of the same car. While in the passenger seat, I have been sending prayers toward heaven for you, Beth and for your family."

Daily after this conversation, Adam and I had talks which included Jesus and His ways, which I was just in the process of learning. Needless to say, we started to develop a bond and we confided a lot in each other. After a few months, Adam related that his marriage was in trouble and he wanted very much for me to meet his wife and convert her.

Whoa—where was this coming from? I hadn't even been able to convert him. For months He tried to contrive ways for this to happen in order to make it appear spontaneous. I kept saying that if it were meant to be, the Lord could orchestrate it without our interference.

My father came home from Texas around this time and he was very ill. After all the testing and probing it was determined that he would have heart bypass surgery.

After his surgery, he was in intensive care in the same hospital where Adam's wife was a nurse. As God would have it, she was one of the nurses who cared for him. For ten days Daddy was there and for ten days I was thrust right in her pathway and developed a friendship with her.

Once again, I am in awe how God arranged for Julie and I to have the perfect opportunity to know one another. I was able to share the times of prayer for Beth and the spiritual awareness that I had seen in Adam and the fact that he was not near as antagonistic toward the things of God as he had once been. Julie and I immediately became kindred spirits. She was very interested in the Kingdom of God and related that she had been a part of the Kingdom in the past. She related her fears of not being "good enough" and ultimately rededicated her life to the Lord.

Back at the ranch—whoops—police station, Adam was learning every day about a new way of living and about the person, Jesus Christ.

One day while sorting out some paperwork, Adam asked about the process of committing your life to Jesus. He said that he thought that he wasn't entirely ready but that he would like to know how to accomplish this when he thought he was better prepared, I told him that there was no way to be properly prepared nor to be "good enough." Right there, Adam bowed his head and accepted Christ asking him to be a part of his life. I was starting to experience what a joy it was to follow the Lord's leading rather than muddle around on my own.

God had a plan and I was starting to appreciate my part in it.

FIVE

Definition – New Creation

2 Corinthians 5:17—Therefore, if anyone is in Christ, he is a new creation; the old has gone, the new has come! (NIV)

One of the magic acts that I was informed would happen to me after acknowledging Jesus was what the "Christians" call transformation. Naturally, if I am told this, and I am sincerely committed to the Lord, I should see it, right? I kept waiting and my attitudes changed somewhat but my demeanor changed very little. My desires didn't change–not at all. My mouth has made an initial attempt to be re-created but believe me when I say I have a long way to go. I am having a difficult time believing that I am OK with God when I am so—not OK— with myself.

At about this time, I have been assigned to work two weeks of the afternoon shift with a Sergeant in order that I might understand the difference between the shifts and ascertain how each shift can benefit the other.

I want you to be able to picture this first evening of work. I am an upbeat, extroverted, fun loving, seldom downcast, person who is very opinionated about those who don't fit into this description. I consider myself serious about my job. At the same time, I value my character and feel it is imperative not to allow the negative factors to consume me.

Imagine my reaction when the Sergeant I am designated to ride with for two weeks is the exact opposite of all of my favorable attributes. (Well, *I* saw them as completely favorable.)

Our first evening in the squad car was extremely reserved. There was not much conversation outside of the particular cases that we were working on at the time. The weather was a good topic. Our children were acceptable conversation, which kept the tone in the vehicle upbeat.

The political workings within the department was a topic that came to the forefront. I immediately realized we could not pursue this subject as it enhanced a negative theme that was outside the realm of my rule of staying positive.

Actually, I soon learned that there were not many topics that did not elicit a negative response and therefore we did not work well together – from my point of view. Three evenings and I was begging the Captain to please assign me with someone else. My plea was denied and I finished working with Sergeant Brandon for the remainder of the two weeks. Shortly thereafter he was transferred to the Detective Division for which I was more than slightly grateful. He was, in my opinion, an unhappy, negatively driven, aggravated, obsessive man.

And did I mention that jokes, jollity and jesting did not fit into his lifestyle?

A short while after Brandon was transferred to the Investigative Division, he came to the Youth Bureau, as was quite common, to visit with fellow officers. I was present at the time. As the other officers left the office to follow up on cases, I was involved in a conversation with Brandon. After our work related conversation ended, he informed me that he and his wife had separated and would I consider going to dinner with him.

My brain immediately said No–No–No! This person did not fit my criteria for a dinner date or any other kind of a date. However, I had bombed big time in relationships where the other person fit my perceived plan. So, before I could complete the thought process, I heard my mouth say "Yes, I would be delighted to go to dinner with you." My reasoning told me that he had already filed for divorce so I was ok.

I told you that I was not even close to transformation yet.

I felt then and I feel now that God meets us where we are and my telling this is in no way a green light for anyone finding him or herself in this position. Nor is it a condemnation for anyone already in this place, in his or her walk with the Lord.

Our friendship continued to grow. I made it a concentrated effort to dispel negative thoughts and actions on Brandon's part. I introduced, not necessarily on purpose, a sense of fun, spontaneity and laughter into his life. He in turn acquainted me with attributes like timeliness, organization, and a few of the more serious sides of living. Together we were really developing the opposite sides of the others character.

For me, there was a completely different texture to this relationship. I had so often cynically approached my relationships living in anger, resentment, and always with an attitude that *this* was going nowhere. At the same time, I left the appearance with others and falsely with myself that I was upbeat and happy.

I now felt that I was developing a close friendship with someone who cared about me, who was different from me, and who did not always abide by the values to which he was accustomed. I knew that he was attracted to me physically but not as the number one priority. This particular attitude was of extreme importance to me at this point in my life.

In spite of my lack of "transformation," I continued to pray for my boys, Brandon, his children, and myself. My boys were very important to me and I wanted them to be considered first in regard to all of my decisions. Of course I wanted God to see how valuable my point of view was also. (Do you think there might be a little room for growth here?) I knew it was difficult to develop a relationship with anyone when the demands of raising two children alone took up so much time and energy.

God is the God of children above and beyond our recognition. The Principal of the school where my boys attended called me and related a story of a family in a nearby city who were interested in testing themselves in regard to involvement in foster care. This family did not want to commit to being foster parents and then not feel able to fulfill that commitment. The Principal was asking if I would consider allowing my boys to spend the summer on a farm with this family. I was reluctant to be away from them for a whole summer but knew that it would be very beneficial to the development of my relationship with Brandon.

The family in conservative Iowa opened their home to the boys. They were a gift from God. I was informed immediately that they would love for me to come and visit whenever I wanted. I did, as often as possible, and the peace and serenity that was present in their home was overwhelming.

One of their daily routines was devotions after every meal. During that time, the devotions were geared toward the age of the boys. Of course, when I was present, these devotions fit well for me, as my knowledge was severely limited.

Brandon's divorce was final in March and we were married in May. My children were exited about being a complete family for the first time that they could remember. They were not used to having a father figure in their lives and it was not always easy for them. They did accept Brandon and did enjoy the family atmosphere that our marriage provided.

Initially our marriage was not accepted well by our peers in the police department. My friends were mainly outside the department and they were very happy for us. His "friends" reminded him often that I was a tarnished, immoral, tainted woman and he was a fool to have sullied his life with me. On their behalf, now, I can see where they were coming from but they were unable to see my heart, a heart that was heeding the guidance of the Lord.

At this time, I was working Juvenile and Brandon was assigned to Investigations. We were asked to work as a team on sexual assault cases and we made a very persistent team on behalf of the investigation of assault cases. Our unity made it possible to combine our characteristics of compassion and objectivity when interviewing both victims and suspects.

By this time, I also saw the need to include God's guidance in all of our efforts as police officers. I had read in the Bible how God felt about His police officers (i.e authority).

Romans 13:1—Everyone must submit himself to the governing authorities, for there is no authority except that which God has established. The authorities that exist have been established by God. (NIV)

Each day I would pray that he would lead my actions and that He would give us the wisdom and knowledge to determine the scope and content of our investigations. I would further ask the Lord to comfort the victims of these horrible circumstances. At the same time, I prayed that the Lord would bring healing to the mind of the perpetrators of such heinous crimes and to deal with them as He willed.

Heck, I amazed myself with such prayers because personally I wanted to just shoot the perpetrators and spare the victim the effort of the inquiry and a possible trial.

Historically, at this time, rape cases were seldom carried through to prosecution. There were many people involved in the process that simply would not acknowledge that rape was even possible. In 1974 - 1975 it was quite common for both males and females to look upon rape as an impossible act. If it was acknowledged that the possibility existed then the victim was portrayed as loose or somehow asked for it. Therefore, in order to pursue a case to a successful end we were up against what seemed to be a gigantic brick wall. I loved the challenge of any form of wall in those days.

With the help of many dedicated people, we helped to set up a Rape Crisis Committee, which in turn began a victim's advocate group. During this process, we were asked to speak before many service-oriented groups to garner support for victims.

Brandon and I spent approximately 4 years working these cases together. We were assigned to many that turned into high profile cases. One of those cases will always be an example for me of the awesome power of God.

Within a radius of approximately 200 miles, our area was plagued with several rapes.

Each of these assaults had a similar modus operandi which means a distinct pattern that indicates or suggests the work of a single criminal in more than one crime and the description of the perpetrator varied very slightly. On the occasions when this occurred in our city, the assailant went twice to a multiple dwelling unit apartment-residence.

As the investigation unraveled, it became apparent that this was not the first time that this suspect had been at this apartment complex. It seemed that he was familiar with occupants other than his proposed victim. After studying the identical cases from other cities, a fact glared off the pages of every Officer's report. This rapist studied his victims and their comings and goings very well. He always picked young females, or at least they looked very young. They also could be described as minutely petite.

In each played-out scenario the assailant came to the door of the victim wearing a white hard hat. He would then inform the female, answering her door that he worked for the city. He then relayed to her that there was a water pressure problem in the area. Could he enter and check the water pressure? Then he kindly requested that she help him determine just how badly this problem existed. He would ask that she go to the bathroom and turn on the water while he did the same in the kitchen. He would then shout questions to her. He would ask if she had the hot water on or the cold. He would seek to determine from her if she still was running the water at its fastest rate. Then he'd request that she turn off the hot and have the cold remain running. During the time that he was making these bellowed requests, he would be rummaging through her kitchen drawers.

After he found a butcher knife he would yell out a couple more demands while he was thanking her for helping in this manner. After this bombardment of questions, he quietly approached the bathroom and grabbed his prey, placing her neck in the crux of his left arm at the elbow and would adorn the other side of her throat with her own butcher knife.

After reaching this level in his fantasy, he would then escort the female into her own bedroom and proceed to rape her. When he had completely violated this girl, he would put a pillowcase over her head and demand that she remain lying in the bed for ten minutes. In at least one case he threatened to kill the children sleeping in the adjoining bedroom if the victim violated the 10-minute limit.

Our city and several others sought this particular perpetrator during a period of one year. Several times we met with Investigation Units of other cities comparing dynamics and pertinent details. Department professionals and also psychology professionals made graphs and profiles.

During the time span of these on-going inquiries of victims, witnesses, and other department details, I happened to be sent on a call to a residence. I was acquainted with the complainant who informed me that she was in the process of divorce from her husband.

She reported that she was very concerned as he had been showing some very disturbing behavior prior to their split-up and since. She related how this man had tied her to the bed and violated her repeatedly by inserting foreign objects into her. She claimed that he continually told of fantasies of having sex with young girls. She recounted times while they were still living together when he would point out girls that he was interested in sexually and they were always very small and very young. This couple had been separated for approximately three months and their divorce was very soon to be final. Without explaining my purpose, I asked this complainant if she had any pictures of her soon-to-be ex-husband that I might see. She very willingly gave me three or four of them.

While listening to the complainant, I started to feel that there could possibly be some connection between her ex and the series of sexual assaults that had been taking place.

Brandon and I shared our suspicions with other agencies and started a preliminary check on this man—Todd.

After looking into his work record, we found that he worked for a local company that through their work could place him in the cities that had reported identical cases. We had an identification team do some surveillance in order to obtain some pictures of this possible suspect that were not given to us by his estranged wife. After obtaining these pictures, they were included with several others pictures of males with similar builds and coloring and shown to victims for possible identification.

Todd was brought in for questioning and was not cooperative in the least. He was eventually arraigned and brought to trial for one sexual assault in our city. It might be mentioned here again that rape was not accepted very readily in those years and it took a great deal of determination on a victim's part to withstand the accusatory questions of the defense attorneys not to mention the not-so-kind inquiries of the prosecution.

Brandon and I took a personal interest in each victim. Not that we automatically believed she was telling the truth, quite the contrary. I learned early on in the questioning of victims that almost always they lied or embellished the truth.

It took two or three sessions of completely retelling the circumstances before the total accuracy of the account was learned. It was normally found that the victims blamed themselves for being in the wrong place at the wrong time or that they may have been dressed in a manner that asked for such a reaction.

The victim in this case had suffered enormously at the hands of the rapist. She had nightmares, questioned all males' motives including her husband and lived in a sense of fear that was impossible for "outsiders" to understand. Her husband not only did not want her to report the incident, he was unable to understand or to sympathize with the emotions and fears that she experienced after the attack.

The family—husband, wife and two small children—moved 400 miles away before the beginning of the trial. Two years went by before the beginning of the formal proceedings. This young victim returned to our city several times at the demand of a subpoena. Upon her arrival, she would find that the fact-finding deposition had been postponed. This young lady had traveled many miles, after having found an appropriate caretaker for her two toddler children. By this time, her husband had left her, as he could not understand the emotional roller coaster that she was forced upon at the point of a knife. She could not find a path out of the maze of this intense, vicious act that held her mind and emotions captive.

Brandon and I were amazed at this young ladies tenacity. She did not waiver in her determination to follow through what she felt was her responsibility in order to save others from the intense hell that she was suffering.

It became apparent to Brandon and I that Rachael could not afford the housing (this was long before victim reparations) in order to continue to return for court proceedings, both genuine and "postponed." Thus we asked Rachael if she would be willing to stay with us during these trying trips.

God's Wisdom and His plan are always perfect and we soon learned that He had a plan for Rachael and for us. We were able to offer to her God's healing Word and His plan of salvation and she offered us His example of hope.

God had already instilled in Rachael the realization that these proceedings were her avenue for healing. She took on the hardships of the trial without complaining knowing that she would reap the benefit of knowing that others would possibly be saved from the same torment. The pain that Rachael experienced was real and you could feel that sorrow with her when she talked. At the same time, she was always considerate of the attorneys involved on both sides of the justice table.

Ultimately the perpetrator was acquitted. Brandon and I were both appalled. Not because of the acquittal, as we believed then and still believe in our justice system. We were horrified with the whole process. Witnesses absolutely essential to the case were not allowed to testify. Evidence that was overwhelmingly necessary was not allowed to be introduced. I believe there was more time spent on evidence suppressions, than the actual trial.

One witness could testify that the perpetrator was in the building minutes before the actual rape. She was kept from giving her account. This perpetrator had attempted, by the same method, to enter her apartment.

Upon leaving the courtroom that day the defendant passed me in the courthouse lobby, sneered at me and said, "I'm gonna kill you."

I went home that day feeling totally defeated and possessing a certain amount of fear. I knew that this man knew where we lived and that he had a degree of anger that could possibly prod him to follow through on his threat. I went to pray, (actually I went to weep, scream and display my anger) regarding the outcome of this trial.

After attempting to appear religious and reverent with God, He impressed on my heart that He indeed was still in control and that His plan was much more righteous than ANY courtroom. He let me know that there was not a court in the universe that would take precedent over the final judgment, which was not mine to determine. I have never forgotten that lesson. Many times in the years that have followed, this revelation has kept me from falling into the pit of emotions that come from seeing injustices in and out of the courtroom.

There are times when I have found that God does not reveal the totality of His plan for quite some time (our time that is).

Ten years later I had been on the night shift for just a couple of weeks. I was in a car by myself and was not yet acclimated to uniform shift work let alone working in the dark. To be bluntly truthful, I was terrified. This was a whole new world for me. I was dispatched to a "Burglary in Progress" to an address in a very nice area of the city. I heard by radio that my cover car was miles and miles away and I on the other hand was only a few blocks from the location. My radio informed me that the homeowner would be in his vehicle in the driveway.

The policy or rule is that you should not enter the residence without your cover car. However, I had seen this rule violated many times in order to apprehend a criminal in the process of committing the crime.

So of course I intended to do the same.

The owner of the residence stepped very slowly from his vehicle, which was parked in the driveway, as I informed the communications operator that I was 10-23 (meaning I had arrived where I had been dispatched).

You know what they say about the dark. Everything appears more dismal in the dark. Well, my headlights were the only things that lit up that driveway and there spotlighted was the perpetrator of 10 years ago. The echo playing in my head went like this: "I'm going to kill you; I'm going to kill you."

I abandoned the notion of searching the house without a cover car. I opened my squad car door and said to him. Take a seat in your car and we will search the house as soon as the second car arrives. This man, whom I am imagining has set this whole scene up, responded by, "Yes, Officer." He immediately abided by the command and went to his car. My cover, which should have taken several minutes to arrive, seemed to arrive in seconds.

The homeowner exited his car and treated us with exaggerated respect. When the search of the home was accomplished, and I was alone to write the report, I pondered on the demeanor of the homeowner and compared that with the young man of ten years earlier. Something or someone had definitely changed his life.

I only know one thing for sure—Jesus is the life changer and I have no idea what occurred in this homeowner's life but I do know it was for the better and thus glorified God in my eyes. I had spent much time praying for both the victim and the perpetrator in this case and God showed me His hand in both lives.

God has a plan no matter who acknowledges their part in it.

SIX

"God – Do You See This?"

Psalm 136:23-24—He remembered us in our low estate. His love endures forever and freed us from our enemies. His love endures forever. (NIV)

Like powdered sugar drifting from the sifter describes a December evening in the mid '70s. Ann parked in the loading zone at a local department store to pick up parcels she had ordered for their family Christmas. The time was after work and she was elated to have left the workplace thinking about a cozy evening in the comfort of home. Parcels in hand, Ann left the store feeling light even with the weight of the packages. She put the packages in the back seat and opened the front door of her vehicle. Her right leg was firmly positioned in the car and she was just about to bring her left leg up when she felt an arm shove her with colossal force to the passenger side of her car.

This wild-eyed individual grabbed Ann by her throat, displaying a knife. He demanded the keys. Ann had them ready to use as she had unlocked the door. She looked over the situation, contemplating an attempt to dart out of the passenger door and realized that it was locked. From where she sat the knife looked like a cleaver rather than a 5-inch blade. This move clearly was out of the question. Ann vacillated between screaming and crying. He threatened to cut her throat if she didn't shut up.

As she was sobbing inwardly, the driver went approximately 3 miles away from the downtown area and parked her car in a relatively quiet neighborhood away from any heavy traffic. Ann again attempted to compose herself enough to form a plan of escape. With his knife at her throat he forced her to unzip his pants and told her to give him oral sex.

The mere thought made her gag and get the dry heaves. He tightened the grip around her neck, digging the knife into her throat and shouted that she obey or the consequences were obvious. Ann attempted to comply and was not completely successful due to gagging.

The perpetrator switched scenarios at this point and demanded that Ann remove her clothes. Her hesitation created a dig in the ribs with his knife.

Ann very slowly started removing her clothes. She started at the top and all the while moving a little closer to the passenger side of the vehicle. He shouted at her to return to his side of the car. She managed to say that she could not remove her apparel without room. As her arms rose to take off her blouse she was able to unlock the passenger door. Ann shivered as much from fear as from the cold.

He yelled at her to hurry up. She managed to slide out of her slacks. He positioned the knife under the back of her bra as she was bent over and cut it off.

The only piece of material that dressed her thin body now was her panty hose. Ann slowly worked at the elastic at her waist convinced that she would escape from this lunatic before she would submit to any further sexual assault. As soon as she had the nylons off her feet, Ann continued to appear as though she were struggling with the process with her left hand as her right grabbed the door handle and she started to exit the car.

He kept grabbing for her and when he realized that he was losing this battle, he swiftly exited the car also.

Confronting Ann at the sidewalk, he started stabbing at her with his knife. Adrenaline consumed Ann and she defended herself by putting her hands in front of her face. All the time Ann was screaming for someone, anyone to help her.

He slipped on the sidewalk and started to fall. Ann took advantage of the brief time he was occupied and ran to the nearest house. She frantically hammered on the door and the occupant opened the door in shock to find there a naked woman.

The occupant looked out into the street very briefly to see the car making a U-turn and heading south. Ann's guardian then covered her with a blanket and called the police.

Ann was transported to the hospital, where the police and many other agencies met her. The cuts she obtained were mostly in the area of her hands as she attempted to shield herself. She had also received a blow to her head and her ear.

Approximately one hour after Ann's horrendous event, May was leaving a local discount store not far from where Ann was filing her report.

May pulled up to the store to get her packages when a white male shoved his way into her car and pulled a knife on her and drove away in her car. The end result, May was brutally assaulted both physically and sexually. He then ran from the scene and left her in her vehicle. May reported the incident but requested that it not be prosecuted nor publicized.

See Pages 102 – 103

The following morning Brandon and I were assigned both cases at roll call. Jeers were sent our way indicating we were dealt all the good cases. At this point, there were no suspects and the description of the perpetrator was fairly vague. We offered to relinquish it and the command officer gruffly indicated that we would do no such thing and that we would accomplish a completed case, meaning there would be an arrest.

We were given May's report as an investigative tool and we did speak to the victim. The most outstanding outcome of our interview was the description of the perpetrator and the MO. These were identical to the case reported by Ann.

Our initial interview with Ann was heartbreaking. She had already repeated her story several times and now, with very little sleep, we were asking her to tell it again.

I called her a trooper as she seldom, if ever, complained. She wrote a very good statement containing detailed accounts of the happenings and reported to us every time she was reminded of another aspect or explicit element that she remembered.

We spent days with Ann rewriting her statement as details were brought back to her remembrance by reliving events of that horrible night. During those days, we silently prayed for Ann and her family. Sexual assault is a destructive experience not only for the victim but also for their entire family. The victim suffers ongoing fear for an unspecified time. Ann would often wake up in the night screaming. She became obsessed with locking doors and windows. She saw perpetrators behind every light post and her family became as paranoid as she at first and later they simply became annoyed.

At some point in this process, we shared that Jesus was in fact the only person who could be with her incessantly and only He could take away her fear. As leads surfaced, we reported them to Ann and we prayed for her and her family daily. The leads were few and far between in this case. Even if we were unable to share details with Ann about May's case, the fact did comfort Ann to know that she was not alone in this process.

Several months went by when another case surfaced with not exact but a lot of similar circumstances.

The time was 2 AM and the location was at a drive-up phone station. Joelle was using the phone after having been out for the evening. Out of the blue, her car door opened and a foot kicked her to the passenger side of the car. The slight young man had a knife and he threatened her with it if she did not quit her incessant screaming. He then shoved his foot onto the accelerator of the already running vehicle. In doing so, he literally ripped the phone cord and receiver off the booth. He then drove to a secluded area in the middle of town and parked the car. He made it clear right from the beginning that he was going to have sex with her.

Joelle tried every conceivable method to keep this from happening. She stalled, conversed, asked questions, sympathized with, and utilized any other deception. Joelle also had the idea that she wanted to obtain as much information as she could in a future attempt to identify him.

At one point she saw something drop from his pocket and she moved it with her foot under the seat to conceal it. This perpetrator's mood ranged from normal talk to absolute rage. During one of her attempts to escape, he bit her very badly on the arm.

He finally accomplished his crime and drove to another location before he left her with her car.

She waited until the following morning to report the incident. Adding the description of the weasel with the manner in which he performed the crime, we were pretty confidant that the same person accomplished the three cases.

Several more months were put into this investigation. Every time we were led to a possible suspect, we would attempt to set up a lineup in order that the victims might view it. More times than I care to mention, they were as disappointed as we were.

One morning, Joelle came running into the police station exclaiming that she had found the perpetrator. Before our asking, she said that she had just driven by a construction site. She related that as she was stopped at a signal light she had seen him working with several other guys. We retrieved May and Ann in an unmarked squad car, took them to the site, where they also picked him out of the group.

An arrest soon followed. The perpetrator was 5'5", white male, approximately 145 lbs with straggly, unkempt blonde hair just as the victims had described. A local artist had done a composite drawing in regard to this individual and he could have posed for the artwork.

He was very belligerent to the uniform officers who arrested him. He laughed at Brandon when he interviewed him in regard to the assaults. He refused to make any statement and he immediately hired an attorney, which ended any further interviews.

The charges were filed and again, the months went by. Justice moves very slowly.

All of the evidence was being sorted and applied in regard to both cases to build the best prosecution possible. We had interviewed a witness in regard to Ann's case who had been right there when she had been abducted from the parking lot. He could remember minute details but was not as positive about others as we would have liked.

We had an Officer—I say that lightly—approach us and encourage us to talk with this witness and coach him to embellish what he did know and lie about what he didn't.

The "Officer" would say things like, "If you just say that he likely did see the short, scraggly blonde hanging around before this happened."

In other words, put words in his mouth. We enlightened him to the fact that we did not intend to win a case by utilizing false witness. He became very angry with us as this was a high profile case and would be heavily covered by the media.

Every time there was some type of court appearance whether it was the arraignment or the actual trial proceeding, he was there outside the courtroom leaving the appearance that he was the assigned officer in the case. On one occasion, Ann asked if that bothered us and we responded that truthfully it was annoying but our recognition would come from God and not from a TV camera.

Prior to an actual court appearance, this perpetrator harassed these girls by phone on several occasions. He would call and tell them that he was going to "get off" and that if they testified against him that he was going to come after them. He left them with bone chilling fear.

It took lots of prayer and uplifting to keep them willing to go through with the prosecution. There were late night calls and later night prayer requests to keep them safe and willing to rid society of a dangerous, dangerous man. The end result, he pleaded guilty to kidnapping and two charges of sexual assault.

During Ann's assault she lost her hearing in one ear, which made the severity even worse. When this was over, all involved were praising God that he was behind bars.

He was sentenced to life in prison. In our state there was no release or parole for persons sentenced to life.

Recently, by accident, we learned that this sadistic individual had made a request of the new liberal Governor for the opportunity to apply for parole.

The Governor granted this possibility. Immediately Brandon set into action a network to inform the Governor and the Parole Board the lengths that this perpetrator went to in order to harass the victims after the horrendous atrocities that were committed against them in the first place.

The victims suffered another few months of fear, and more prayer was sent to the Father before we would hear the outcome.

Before the fear and pain would end again for the victims, they would be asked to appear before the parole board to testify to the circumstances regarding each case. We were told by one of the victims that this process was also a part of the healing for her. God is definitely a part of every plan.

The Lord heard our prayers and although the parole board was allowed to hear the case, they chose to leave him locked up. Thank God for His plan and our ability to be a part of it.

SEVEN

Am I Really Blind?

John 9:25—He replied, "Whether he is a sinner or not, I don't know. One thing I do know. I was blind but now I see!" (NIV)

Jodi left home very light-hearted. Her best friend Martha came to pick her up dressed for a night on the town. Jodi, simply dressed, was not out to impress anyone. She had a new two-month-old baby girl. Her husband had been away driving truck since the baby's birth.

Jodi's Mom had come to visit and encouraged her to go with Martha to get a break from the everyday stress.

The girls went to The Chamber, a local bar. While there, they ran into Martha's boyfriend, Joe. After spending approximately an hour visiting, Joe suggested that they go to another local nightspot. This entertainment location was thought of as a country western bar and was welcomed by Jodi as she really enjoyed country music.

A friend of Joe's joined them and visited for a while. After a few drinks, Jodi remarked to Martha that she would like to go home. Martha was enjoying her time with Joe. She related to him that Jodi would like to go home and he suggested that they go to a local truck stop for a bite to eat and then go home.

Vince, Joe's friend, asked if he could tag along as he had enough to drink and would appreciate getting some food. Martha was driving and agreed to the food program.

In route to the truck stop they drove through a State Park. This was a short cut according to Vince. When they pulled into the park Vince suggested that he and Jodi go for a walk in order that Joe and Martha could spend some time alone. Jodi agreed, as the weather was a perfect picture of autumn.

Jodi could not remember well how far they had walked when Vince grabbed her and tried to kiss her. She avoided the kiss and told him that under no terms was she looking for this type of treatment. Jodi, talking through a damaged mouth, informed us the next morning that Vince completely went berserk. She says she could just remember him repeatedly punching her.

Jodi recalled that when she came to, the first thing she realized was that she had no clothing on. She could not see and was in a panic as she thought she was blind. She said that she started feeling around on the ground, among the fallen leaves.

She found her underclothing and her pants and shirt. Her bra had been torn in two. Jodi also had no idea where she was in relation to the car. She just crawled until she came upon an area, which did not seem to have any trees. She bumped into a car and crawled up onto the trunk and started banging on it. Jodi was not at all certain whose vehicle this was.

The couple, in the back seat of the car, was frightened when they heard something banging on the car. They exited the car to find Jodi lying behind it. Joe and Martha thought perhaps Jodi had come in contact with some type of animal. Jodi had, in fact, come in contact with the worst type of animal. His name was Vince. They immediately took her to the hospital.

I have seen worst things in my career, but not at the hand of a rapist. When Brandon and I went to the hospital to interview Jodi the following morning, she still could not see and she said to me, "Am I blind?"

Her eyes were completely swollen shut. She was bleeding from both ears. Reliving the events of the previous evening included a description of the assailant. Jodi described him as a nice looking man of about 5' 9" who obviously was a body builder as he was very muscular.

Jodi's physical condition was apparent. However, along with her bruises she wore giant guilt, claiming that if she had remained at home, she would not be in the hospital but instead she would be at home with her baby daughter. Jodi kept saying that she should not have gone out. She said, "If I had stayed home, none of this would have happened." If the circumstances had not been so serious I would have simply replied, "Duh".

I made it a priority to pray for Jodi's quick recovery in order that she hastily be returned to her family. Later in the day when she was dismissed from the hospital she came to the station to be photographed by the Identification Unit. I remember looking at a photograph of a very large head with no distinguishable features and her face was mostly black and blue. I was amazed, days later, when Jodi came into the department to view some photos in hopes of identifying her assailant. She was a very pretty girl with a thin face and very pretty features, which included a freckled nose.

An interview with Martha and Joe revealed exactly who Vince was. After the viewing of a photo line up, Jodi pointed out the individual that she knew as Vince. We found that he had been arrested on previous assault charges. We found his construction workplace and a home address.

We were unable to find him at either location. More detective work revealed that he had family in California. With the help of relatives, we found that he had fled to Loma Linda, California. Charges were filed relative to the case of State vs. Vince and a warrant was issued for Vince. Due to the seriousness of the case, extradition was a possibility and a call was made to the California city. Brandon and another law enforcement officer traveled to California and brought Vince back in cuffs.

Lives are touched by all who come in contact with a Spirit-filled person, including the Spirit-filled person herself. This was one of the cases that I was the most angry about during my 25 year career. Jodi accepted blame for a crime that she did not commit. I was knowledgeable enough to know that God did not send this kind of evil to Jodi.

Jodi was more than certain that Vince would never be found and he would never have to take responsibility for this rape. No matter how much I tried to tell her, she could not get through the blame thing. I finally had to give in which I should have done in the first place—and pray that God would take control and deal with my unbelief at the same time.

Now, God is not a magician to answer our crystal ball wishes. However, He does His will and if your will matches His, your answer will always be yes—in His time.

My desire to share this story is not to tell another morbid event but to say that even in the most horrid times of our lives, God is there to lead us to the car that we might bang on the trunk as in Jodi's case. He is there to lead us to a rapist who has fled to the other side of the country. He is even there to meet out justice even when *we* disagree with the *justice* that the world sometimes offers.

In this set of circumstances, when the case came before the preliminary Judge, he dismissed the rape charge because the victim was unconscious and could not testify to the actual act.

The defendant was bound over to District Court for Assault with Intent to Commit Manslaughter. He pleads guilty and the Judge sentenced him to 1 year in the county jail. He was immediately out on work release. He also immediately walked away from work release for a day or two.

Jodi's courage may have saved another young lady from a similar fate. God does have a plan. He wants us to be part of it.

EIGHT

Is There A Reason I May Not Live In A Safe Bubble?

Matthew 6:14—For if you forgive men when they sin against you, your heavenly Father will also forgive you. (NIV)

So one morning I was assigned an abuse/neglect case. After the completion of the interviews with the family members, it was determined that this was directed only at the 12-year-old daughter, named Machelle.

Machelle was a beaming, happy faced, fragile appearing young girl. The naked eye would never be able to identify her as a victim of serious physical abuse.

During each and every interview, I came away enraged. I was angry with the mother who had been told that this was going on. The verbal abuse was performed in the mother's presence. The daughter told how she didn't want to go home from school each night as she knew that whatever frustrations her father had would be taken out on her. He had been ill and the mother had been forced to work more and more hours and thus the daughter was home alone with him.

The responsibility for more and more of the housework and the father's care was given to her. The young girl related how she tried to get up early in the morning and leave the house before the father was up for the day in order that she wouldn't have to see him. Then how she would be in so much trouble when she returned home, usually because she didn't help him with something that he needed to have done before she left for school?

His abuses were mixed with minute signs of affection that Machelle craved. It was hard for her to separate the good from the bad. He would grab her and smack her around because she did not have a meal prepared to his liking.

This man was (at this point) bed-ridden and so Machelle would have to get close to him to care for him. When he asked for anything it was with kindness and consideration and when she did not deliver with his expediency, or in the same manner in which he would have accomplished it, he would find deviant ways to abuse her.

The see-saw effect had gone on for many months for Machelle when she passed a note to a friend and her teacher intercepted it. The teacher in turn reported the case to the police.

My interviews with Machelle were painful for me. I was livid to think that a grown man would mistreat a 12-year-old girl to this extent especially when she was trying so hard to please and care for him.

One evening during the course of this investigation, my sister, her husband and my family were having a very informal dinner. As we were visiting, I related to my sister how outrageously nervy I thought child abuse perpetrators were. I then referred to some of the facts of the current case without being specific.

When I finished my tirade, my sister looked at me somewhat stunned and said, "Why are you speaking as though these are fresh facts to you? Why is this any different than our childhood home? You were that little girl."

The hospitality ended for me at that point as reality came crashing in on me. She was 100% accurate and I had lived in denial for 33 years, pretending that we had the only functional home in the tri-state area. I went to my room. I wept with the realization that I had been brutally abused by my Father.

At the same time that I whitewashed his behavior, I openly projected the fact that I hated him. If a conversation arose which included a reference to my dad, I most willingly told anyone listening that I hated him. I knew this was not acceptable to God but I did not want to do the one thing necessary to change it either.

I knew that in order for God to correct the horrible feelings that I had due to years of hatred, resentment, and bitterness toward Dad I needed to confess this to him and ask for his forgiveness.

Ha! This was a man who beat me whenever he could conjure up a reason to do so. Believe me, he had plenty of reasons, without fabricating them and he made up scenarios to add to his already plentiful motives for physical attacks.

Nevertheless, I would not be left to rest until I made the call that corrected my attitude about this whole situation. I picked up the phone and called my Father. He answered the phone. I stammered and stuttered before I was able to confer to him that I had harbored years of resentment and bitterness for things that had happened in my childhood. I said that I didn't think that it was necessary to review them. Mostly, I told him that I wanted his forgiveness. His response was, "What the hell are you talking about!" and *BANG,* he hung up.

My natural inclination, after receiving this type of response, would be additional bitter feelings to add to my already varied collection. On this occasion, however, I only felt tranquil, serenity, what a wonderful feeling. It is hard to imagine that obedience to the will of God can bring such peace. Not only did it bring peace but also I was able to then face and truly forgive my Father (even if he didn't acknowledge it).

And, due to my confrontation, which apparently he accepted, as he then came to my house every time he came back to our city which was home to him, even though he lived in another state, and he probably stayed a lot longer than I would have liked. He was always a little confrontational (in other words, he liked to argue) and I even learned to love that.

This whole set of circumstances also made it easier to continue my investigation of child abuse cases. I was able to talk with the perpetrators with a genuine love that comes from understanding that something in them has malfunctioned in order that they should do something so horrid.

In the case mentioned above, the Father initially denied to me any such treatment and made that 12-year-old girl out to be the biggest liar, tramp, and an all-around no good person. After I showed him compassion for his illness and offered him help in the event that he needed emotional support due to being bedridden, he confessed that he had been abusing her both verbally and physically. I offered them counseling but first of all I offered them Jesus. They accepted both.

God has a plan, and it works in spite of our ignorance.

NINE

Younkers has an Angel

Hebrews 1:14—Are not all angels ministering spirits sent to serve those who will inherit salvation?

This is the time of year that I love the most. The leaves have vacated the trees and they have been covered with frosting of cool white. Of course it is also the time when we start to contemplate the season of Christ's birth and all the festivities that seem to connect themselves to the surrounding dates on the calendar.

The actual date was late November and I was talking with my Sergeant, Nathan. I was relating to him that I believed that God sends angels to watch over us and to minister to us, quoting the scripture, *Hebrew 1:14—"Are not all angels ministering spirits sent to serve those who will inherit salvation?"*

I want you to know that I was met with much hostility. I was told that I was carrying the spiritual thing too far. I had told him of a time not long before this when my husband and I were very discouraged and felt very much alone. We were driving to see our son who was in the hospital in another state.

As you would imagine, since we were both involved in law enforcement, we would *never* pick up a hitchhiker. We did make an exception, however, on one occasion. For some unknown reason, when we saw this young man with his thumb out, and no duffel bag or other luggage, we just stopped and picked him up. He said that he was going into the town where we were headed.

We had approximately 40 miles of travel left. Imagine our surprise when this young man introduced himself as a young Christian man by the name of Doug and he spent the entire 40 miles encouraging us. I cannot remember now one word Doug said, but I do remember we arrived at our destination and let Doug out of our car as we entered the city.

We looked around as we pulled away from the side of the road and neither Brandon nor I could see where he had gone. Doug was nowhere to be seen. Before he entered our car, our mental states which had been floating around in the sewer somewhere, were now uplifted. We were not looking back but looking forward to the great things that God intended to do with our lives.

I always wondered if Doug was actually God's Angel of Encouragement.

Nathan's hostility did not hinder me from sharing my great faith in Jesus or in His willingness to send angels to minister to us—if we needed them. Often times I felt that angels protected me at accident sites and at potential accident locations.

So a month before Christmas, I asked Nathan what he was going to give his wife for Christmas. He very abruptly said, "Absolutely nothing."

I told him that I was totally astounded. I had perceived that he was very much in love with his wife and that he held her in very high regard.

He said, "I am in love with her, and I do think of her highly but I refuse to fight the crowds and scramble for a place to park during the Christmas holiday season."

Well, immediately I thought this problem had a simple solution. So I said, "Nathan, this is not a complicated issue and you can still get your wife a Christmas gift." (This was before the shopping mall) I then suggested that when he left the station and headed for home that he pray and ask God to allow him to find a parking space right outside the door of the department store where he would like to purchase his wife a gift.

Needless to say, he told me this was a gigantic bunch of hooey and that he would continue his practice of not buying his spouse a Christmas gift. I just encouraged him then to try and practice his faith. I said that if he believed that God was the answerer of our prayers, he should at least ask.

»

The next morning Nathan came to work. He was just grinning from ear to ear. I laughed and I said, "You asked God for a parking space, didn't you?" He said, "Yep." And I asked, "What was His answer?" Nathan coyly replied, "One right in front of the door."

I was just thrilled. My spirit was jumping up and down and I kept saying, "I told you, man. God is good. He cares about His people and even about the little things." I started to head for my office.

Nathan spoke up and said, "Don't you want to hear the rest?"

I replied, "I'm all ears".

Nathan then told how he went into the department store and headed to the second floor. He intended to buy his wife a pantsuit. He knew exactly what she liked and he knew he would be able to pick one out in short order. He said that a young twentyish brunette came and asked if she could help him. He told her what he was looking for and she told him to have a seat over near the column, she would bring him a few in the color and style that he had described.

She was gone a very short time and came back with three or four pantsuits. One of them was just perfect. She told him to take it to the register and she would return the rest of the pantsuits. Upon finishing the transaction at the cash register, Nathan asked the cashier where the pretty brunette might be found, as he wanted to thank her for helping him. The blonde cashier said, "I'm sorry, I am the only one working in this department this afternoon." Nathan relied, "Well then she must have come from downstairs as I know there was a young 20-something brunette who waited on me. She brought me this pantsuit."

The cashier looked at him totally befuddled and said, "Sir, I'm sorry but the lady that works downstairs in women's clothing is 65 years old and all gray so I know it wasn't she."

Nathan told me a light bulb came on and he thought, That brunette doesn't even work in that store, she works for God.

In one November afternoon, God revealed himself to Nathan by answering his prayer for a parking space. He then sent an angel to him to make his first Christmas shopping experience for his wife a pleasant one. God's messenger has touched Nathan and indeed I was touched.

I have really tried to include in my storytelling the "good outcome stories" and especially those that include the aspect of "making me look good." Well, I have been convicted to add this to the current chapter as it involves Nathan.

Shortly after Nathan had come to the realization that God really was real and that we could actually talk with Him and receive answers to our prayers, we had another type of incident occur between us, this one not quite as positive. My family had just moved into a different house and we needed to get our phone installed.

We had waited two weeks for the local phone company to come and I had asked for the day off in order to be there while they did the installation work. Nathan was my immediate supervisor and he had told me no. I did not have a large workload and I had asked for an explanation and I had been refused one. I was immediately incensed. I felt again as though I was being discriminated against because I was the only female in the department and if one of the guys had asked for the day off or whatever time it took to accomplish this task it would have been granted.

My next thought was that there wasn't a guy there who would take a portion of a day to oversee the installation of the phones. That was the wife's job.

At any rate, I solved the problem by calling in sick the following morning. And – to be truthful, I did not think a thing of it—until the next day.

When I arrived at work the following day, Sgt. Nathan immediately said, "I thought you indicated that you were a good Christian person and I have no recourse but to believe that you purposely lied when you called in sick yesterday."

Everything in me wanted to strike back and rationalize my actions. However, I immediately knew that all the witnessing and sharing that I had done over the past several months had been undone by one very selfish act. I was instantly convicted and I confessed that I was wrong and that I should not have done that no matter how I felt about his motives and reasons.

In like manner, he admitted that he had no reason not to have given me the day off and that all was forgiven. I learned a great lesson that day about honesty and integrity. Does that mean that I have not fallen in that area of my life since? Heavens no, but I also recognize immediately when God nudges me and says, "We need to revisit these areas in your life again."

God had a plan—I accept His teaching.

TEN

Whose Side Are You On Anyway?

Titus 1:15—To the pure, all things are pure, but to those who are corrupted and do not believe, nothing is pure. In fact, both their minds and consciences are corrupted. (NIV)

Even though I left the impression that I understood the working of this world and even indicated that I was quite capable of handling the events that came my way, I was quickly learning that this simply was not true. Even in 1976 when things were much calmer than they are now (2002) I am appalled at the animal nature of the creatures that frequent the establishments, way into the wee hours of the morning.

Let me tell you about one of these low-life creatures. For the sake of this story, I am going to call him, Elmer.

The time is very early morning in April. Marissa is a college student who is tending bar in a combination restaurant/lounge in the heart of the city. When the bars close, this is THE place to go to have a late bite to eat before going home to pass out. While everyone else is concerned with ordering the wonderful Italian

Cuisine, Marissa is concerned with "getting home". Normally she calls a cab as she does not drive and has never owned a car.

On this particular morning, Elmer offers to give her a ride home. Two or three weeks prior to this, Elmer had offered Marissa and a friend a ride home after work and he was very cordial and did not give them a hard time, in any respect. Marissa saw no harm in accepting his offer.

After being in Elmer's vehicle for a short period of time, it seemed to Marissa that he was not taking a route to her address. He stopped his truck on a muddy road. He said that he was having some problems with the truck. He got out of the drivers side of the vehicle. Marissa assumed to check out the problem. He came around the truck, opened the passenger door, grabbed her legs and pulled her part way out of the truck. She gave a blood-curdling scream and with that he slugged her several times. He then unsnapped her dress, took off her panty hose and underwear and raped her.

Now, in order to prove that he was a true gentleman, he took her to a location of her choice. She asked to be dropped off at a friend's house, as she did not want to drop this bombshell on her parents. She had certainly given them enough grief in her short 19 years, and she was naturally assuming that this was her fault. After all, she did agree to the ride home.

From the friend's home uniform police officers were called and an investigation was started. Marissa was taken to the hospital. Prior to their arrival in an attempt to wash away the filthy feeling of someone's forced bodily secretions, and all the emotional violations that this crime entails, Marissa could not wait to get into a shower. In doing so the only elements carried down the drain were the valuable pieces of hard evidence that linked Elmer to the sexual assault. The physical, emotional and other trauma was still left clinging to her towel wrapped body. Normal gathering of evidence occurred as well as photos of her face and body bruises. Marissa had taken an object from the perpetrator's truck in the hopes of it being used as a means of getting fingerprints of her assailant. Unfortunately prints were unable to be removed from the item.

At the culmination of our investigation, Elmer was arrested on 5/20/1976. A preliminary hearing was set for 6/10/1976; it was continued to 6/19/1976. In the meantime, the defendant was bound over to the next session of the Grand Jury.

The Grand Jury indicted Elmer on July 13, 1976. The District Court Trial would not occur until May, 1977.

»

During the times that the victim and her mother met with the county attorney's office in the process of preparing for the charging of and the preparing for the court proceedings, the county attorney himself and his assistants many times suggested that she did not have a case. They tried aggressively to dissuade her from going to trial with this case insinuating that she had a sordid past and that "things" would be brought up that she would rather not have "aired in public". On one occasion Marissa was asked if she would be willing to allow Elmer to plead to Simple Assault. She asked why he couldn't just plead to Assault with Intent to Commit Rape and the County Attorney told them that the penalty was the same as Rape.

In the time between the Grand Jury hearing and the District Court Trial, the Defense attorney requested that the VICTIM take a polygraph exam. Marissa gladly agreed to do this IF the perpetrator would agree to do the same thing.

On a personal level, we became well acquainted with Marissa and her family. There was absolutely no one in those days to be advocates for sexual assault victims. In the eyes of the major population of our society, at that time, if a girl was raped, she was either in the wrong place, dressed inappropriately, rebelling, or just plain asking for it. Everyone knows that women want it as much as men. These were all the responses that I heard continually in the early '70s. No one then wanted to acknowledge that rape was about aggression and violence and degradation toward women.

»

Marissa had been through much turmoil in her teen years and this was one more added emotional burden for her to carry. She had caring parents who searched out every avenue to assure that she get the help that she needed to overcome alcohol and drug addictions that she had wrestled with since her high school years. Of course we introduced them to the concept that Jesus was alive and well and able to deliver Marissa from alcohol, drugs and any other evil that the enemy of her soul might attempt to stack upon her. I always said that I would pray that Jesus would have control in Marissa's life, I also explained to Marissa how that control would absolutely come about by simply surrendering her life to Jesus, acknowledging his death on the cross for her sake, and confessing Him as her Savior and asking

Him to take control of a life of which she had no control. Marissa was always so polite, would always listen so intently, and then I would feel the dismissal. So – I would go on my way and pray some more.

Always I would tell her Mom that I would continue to pray for Marissa and their family. I knew that the basics had been taught, as they were a church going Catholic family that took their faith very seriously.

During the court processes, my husband and I spent many hours explaining the procedures and what happens next and if that did not take place what might take place as plan B. As the months progressed, so did my size as I was due to have a baby in December 1976. You might say that Marissa's family was with us through the majority of the pregnancy. Marissa was exceptionally fond of children. She was a very busy college student who often spent weekends and entire weeks with other's children in order that they might attend to business or pleasure. When this entire nightmare was over she offered to do the same for us and thus our relationship continued on a personal level.

»

Our daughter was born in December of 1976. Marissa was around often to see her and to lavish her with gifts. There were times when Marissa would take Stacy for the afternoon when I was off work in order that I might have some much appreciated alone time. I was always impressed with the candor that Marissa displayed. The truth was the truth and you were going to hear it whether you liked it or not – even if it included something that she had just done. I often did not approve but I couldn't disapprove without showing my appreciation for her truthfulness.

Let's fast forward to January 1978. Stacy is one year old. Christmas is just over and we have just completed the large family gathering. I had been trying for a couple of years to convince myself that I had not married an alcoholic – my second marriage – my second alcoholic.

When God gives us the opportunity to put something together – in this case our marriage – He gives us the step-by-step instructions on how to handle relationships and situations and many other concerns. Well, I was seeking God and I was trying to get a grasp on how to – but I was trying to do this on my own. So instead of praying for my husband and asking God to lead me on his behalf, I was brow beating him with what a terrible husband and father he was turning out to be and a lot of ways in which he could improve on those roles. Heck, I didn't even have my own role outlined yet. I continued on in this manner though until I convinced Brandon to join a chemical dependency treatment facility for alcohol abuse. He went very reluctantly and was bordering on "I'd rather leave home than comply."

Brandon had been in treatment for one week when Marissa's mother called me at work on a Saturday morning in an absolute panic. Marissa had been at a "party" the night before where alcohol and drugs were flowing freely and she passed out from overuse. While she was without use of her faculties, someone removed a two-carat diamond ring from her finger. A very close friend had given this ring to her and Marissa's mother was not as concerned with the ring as she was about what was happening with Marissa and where she was headed. I confided in Marissa's mother about Brandon's being in the treatment facility and that if Marissa was willing to go, that I would be glad to take her and get her checked in. That afternoon Marissa and a friend walked into the same treatment facility and checked into the program. I am happy to say that there she met another close friend of ours, Gloria, and they became friends as well.

In the years that have followed, Marissa has accepted the Lord and his control. She has a very simple approach to life. She loves people and will work overtime to help anyone who is willing to work overtime to help themselves. She has two wonderful children that she is raising alone, after the death of her husband, with Jesus as the centerpiece of their lives.

God's plans are perfect with and without our participation.

ELEVEN
This Could Have Been Chapter One

Romans 8:28—And we know that in all things God works for the good of those who love him, who have been called according to his purpose. (NIV)

I have to get back to Gloria, from Chapter 10. When I began the search for a new career, actually I was belly aching a lot about my current career, and not doing much searching. Gloria was the friend who told me that the city was looking for a Police Matron. Her brother worked for the Police Department.

Gloria and I had gone to high school together and had been socializing (both good and bad) for about five years at this point. The major common denominator in our socializing effort was going to bars and drinking and dancing the night away. Through her suggestion and encouragement I followed the process to begin my law enforcement career. There were many times after that fateful set of events, that I would lay awake at night and wondered if Gloria were friend or foe.

I want to put one thing in print right here and now. Gloria was my friend before, she was my friend then and she is my friend today. I wish I could tell this in its entirety but then I would have to write another whole book. So I will try to keep the facts centered on the period of time involving my police career.

A few years after I became a police officer, Gloria married the Assistant Chief of Police. They had a small intimate wedding, which included only family and wedding attendants. Afterward they had a reception at their home, which I attended. We had a great time celebrating and of course we had plenty of food and alcohol. Brandon was very timid about being a part of this social occasion, as well as other social events, which included Chief Hank, as he saw the Assistant Chief as a Command Officer. I saw him mainly as a friend since he was my friend's husband.

When Brandon and I married, they were our wedding attendant's and my very closest friends. We had a very small wedding and then had a very large alcohol soaked celebration immediately following the ceremony. My purpose for detailing this is to acquaint you with the fact that a lot of alcohol was always invited to our celebrations. I was not able to handle it as well as others or should I say sustain consciousness as long as others. It seemed that after a few (4 or 5) I was just instantly out. The rest of our group of friends could party for hours and still be on their feet. At the time I was miffed because I thought I was missing all the fun, later I was grateful.

Gloria's husband left the department and ran for Sheriff. She worked hard and long on his campaign. Like all wives of elected officials, she attended all of the fundraisers and social events necessary to accomplish winning the election. The use of alcohol as the social drink of choice was then, as it is now, used extensively. He served as Sheriff in our county for three years. He then lost the election. Not long after his last term as Sheriff, Hank became ill. It was discovered that he had cancer and it was increasingly apparent that he was not given much hope. Gloria's brother and I were part of the Police Department's prayer group and we were praying for him daily. We were also praying for strength for Gloria, as we knew that she loved him more than life itself and that she gained a great deal of her strength from him.

Hank was finally admitted to the hospital. I had a small baby at home and occasionally I would take her to see him. He loved babies and he was always (or left the appearance of being) upbeat when he had visitors. On one occasion when I went to see him, I knew that I had to talk with him about knowing the Lord. I didn't even have enough knowledge at this point to lead anyone intelligently through a salvation prayer. I know that he listened and I have faith to believe that he is waiting in heaven for Gloria and all of his friends who will heed God's call to simply repent and believe in His Son, Jesus and that He died on the cross that we might have everlasting life with Him.

Hank left his earthly home in April 1977, leaving Gloria feeling very alone. She took care of day-to-day things in an absolute daze and later would say that she did not remember getting through most of those days. After the first few months of getting affairs back in order, the everyday tasks became mundane again. Gloria started drinking at her home on a daily basis. Her parents had moved into her home with her to help stall off the loneliness and it seemed to just fan the flames. On one hand she wanted isolation and on the other hand, she just wanted Hank and no one or anything else would take his place. So she continued to drink.

On several occasions, Gloria's brother would talk with me about his concern. I shared his distress but would tell him that I did not feel that I could interfere unless she asked for help, but I could pray. I prayed like I had never prayed for anything before in my life. Gloria encouraged me continually when I was at my lowest. She lifted my spirits when I made terrible mistakes, told me about them bluntly without trying to make me feel stupid. She was my definition of a friend.

One wonderful day, Gloria called and said that she needed help that she had been drinking way too much and would I help her get into a treatment program. Well, didn't I just know a perfect one; Brandon and Marissa were already there. You know the rest of the story. The details we will leave between the participants but God has a plan and it works according to our willingness and His timing

JOE M. KRIGSTEN, M. D.
MILTON O. GROSSMAN, M. D.

1709 PIERCE STREET   SIOUX CITY, IOWA

May 12, 1972

Chief William Hanson
Sioux City Police Dept.
Municipal Bldg.
Sioux City, IA

Dear Chief Hanson: RE: JANELL RAGER

Dr. Marriott gave us the reports on this applicant's x-rays
as of May 5, 1972. The following is the report: "Cervical spine
shows a very minimal loss of the curve. Dorsal spine shows an
early scoliosis to the left in lower dorsal region and minimal
degenerative changes on the dorsal vertebrae. Lumbo-sacral spine
shows satisfactory alignment, there are minimal degenerative
changes. There is noted an interuterine device."

This applicant is showing arthritic changes in the spine which
at the present time are not causing her any difficulty. The outlook for this applicant is that there will be good probability of
disability in about a ten year period.

At the present time her examination shows her to be fit for
employment, but I strongly recommend that before she be admitted
to the pension service that she should be examined at least a
month prior to her being admitted to the pension plan.

Yours very truly,

J. M. Krigsten

JMK:ss

91

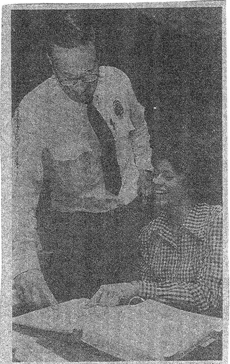

Police training officer Lt. Ronald Pettit discusses the day's lesson with Mrs. Janell Rager, Sioux City's first woman police officer. 1972

First Woman Police Officer in Training

Mrs. Janell Rager, Sioux City's first woman to be classified as a police officer, has started her eight weeks of basic training with a class of 12 other recruits, all men.

Mrs. Rager, the mother of two young sons, said that she accepted the appointment to the police department because "the work would be a challenge." Mrs. Rager formerly was an executive secretary for Terra Chemicals.

Mrs. Rager was reared on a farm near Hinton and attended Sioux City schools.

SIOUX CITY GRADUATES RECRUITS

These men and one woman graduated July 7, 1972 from the Sioux City Police Academy recruit training. The men in blue have been assigned to all divisions and the woman to the youth bureau. Front row from left: Raymond Cota, Woodbury County Sheriff's Office; Peter Groetken; Anthony Sunclades; Larry Wilcox; Janell Rager; Douglas Benton; Terry Murkins; and David Ingalls, Woodbury Sheriff's Office. 2nd row: Lt. Ronald Pettif, instructor; David Hansen; Herb Fischer; Tim Blum; Milton Olson, Jr.; Pat Burke; Mike Post; and Bill Enockson.

JOE M. KRIGSTEN, M. D.
MILTON D. GROSSMAN, M. D.

1709 PIERCE STREET   SIOUX CITY, IOWA

April 12, 1973

Chief William H. Hansen
Sioux City Police Department
Municipal Building
Sioux City, Iowa

                    Re: Janell Rager

Dear Chief Hansen:

I have your memo of March 29, 1973 to Janell Rager in regard to
this policewoman and her examination for admittance to the Pension
Fund.

I believe that this letter is to be taken by you to the Pension
Board.

At the time of her first examination on 5-5-72, the report by
Dr. Marriott was as follows: "Cervical spine shows a very minimal
loss of the curve. Dorsal Spine shows an early scoliosis to the
left in the lower dorsal region and minimal degenerative changes
of the dorsal vertebrae. Lumbo-sacral spine shows satisfactory
alignment, minimal degenerative changes. There is noted an interuterine device."

On May 12, 1972, I also recommended that when the time came for
her pension service, she should be re-evaluated at least prior to
her being admitted to the pension plan.

The following is the report of 4-2-73 of x-rays taken at our office
and which were read by Dr. L. E. Collins: "Studies of the cervical
spine show very minimal straightening of the curve. Cervical spine
is otherwise negative. Views of the thoracic spine show very
minimal S-deformity at the level of T-7 with curvature to the left
at this level. Thoracic spine and rib cage otherwise negative.
Views of the lumbar spine show scoliosis to the right. Lumbar spine
is otherwise negative."

94

Chief William H. Hansen   April 12, 1973
Re: Janell Rager

My personal opinion is the same as it was at first; that this
policewoman will probably have some disabling symptoms within the
next ten-year period. This is based on our past experience and
the probability or possibility of having had these symptoms. It
may be that she will not be disabled during that time but this
should be considered in admitting her to the Pension Group.

                   Yours very truly,

                   Joe M. Kragsten, M. D.

JMK:hb

LAW OFFICES

HARRY H. SMITH

April 19, 1973

632-636 BADGEROW BLDG.
SIOUX CITY, IOWA 51101
TELEPHONE (712) 255-8094
RESIDENCE (712) 277-3368

South Dakota Office
ROBERT O'CONNOR, RESIDENT ATTORNEY
Suite 907 National Bank of South Dakota Bldg.
100 N. Phillips Ave.
Sioux Falls, South Dakota 57102
Telephone (605) 336-1564

Chief William Hansen
Sioux City Police Department
Municipal Building
Sioux City, Iowa

Dear Mr. Hansen:

Re: <u>Officer Janell Rager</u>

It is my understanding that Officer Rager has been informally advised that she will not receive permanent status because of a back condition which existed at the time of her employment.

Officer Rager has requested that I represent her and such representation has been approved by the Sioux City Policemen's Association whom I am advised feel generally she has been an excellent officer.

Further, I am advised by Officer Rager that you have already advised her that the sole reason for her failure to achieve permanent status is the physical problem.

I also note that Dr. Joe Kirgsten's report does not indicate any worsening of the condition over the past year. In fact his last letter is quite inconclusive in that it ends with this statement:

"It may be that she will not be disabled during that time but this should be considered in admitting her to the Pension Group."

In representing Officer Rager I am fully aware that no reason need generally be given for a dismissal during a probationary period.

LAW OFFICES

HARRY H. SMITH

612-616 BADGEROW BLDG.
SIOUX CITY, IOWA 51101
TELEPHONE (712) 255-8094
RESIDENCE (712) 277-3258

South Dakota Office
ROBERT O'CONNOR, RESIDENT ATTORNEY
Suite 907 National Bank of South Dakota Bldg.
100 N. Phillips Ave.
Sioux Falls, South Dakota 57102
Telephone (605) 336-1584

Chief William Hansen   page 2   April 19, 1973

However, when one is given and if that reason is either constitutionally impermissible or a "pretext" for a constitutionally impermissible reason then such action is contrary to law. See: 42 U.S.C.A, Section 1983 (Civil Rights Statute) and the many cases thereunder.

Absent a worsening of Officer Rager's back condition which is not indicated, it appears that such is a "pretext" to cover an unconstitutional dismissal based on the sex of Officer Rager.

Many male officers have received waivers for physical deficiencies. None have ever been dismissed for physical problems that existed at the time of their hire if such problems did not worsen.

This letter is being written in the hope that the whole issue may be reconsidered without the necessity of resorting to a federal court action which may in fact be the only legal avenue available to Officer Rager in view of the statutory year probationary period which bars any appeal to the Civil Service Commission and perhaps even any formal appeal to the City Council.

I would be pleased to meet either with you or the city attorney to discuss the matter as would also the Sioux City Policemen's Association.

Sincerely,

Harry H. Smith

Harry H. Smith

HHS/bh

c/c's: Mayor Paul Berger
       Councilman Bill Gross
       Councilman Jan Abertson
       Councilman Bill Cole
       Councilman Howard Weiner
       City Attorney
       Civil Service Commission (4 copies)

Janell C. Armstrong

DDRESS   D College Court;   C ity 51106
. r.   Police Department
. B.   Dr. Wiedemeier
:S :

AGE: 31   3-14-42

PHONE: 276-8437

X RAY #

*Patient consents to a report to Dr. Wiedemeier only and signs no authorizatio
for report to anyone else.*

C. C. -   Pain in the low back when doing heavy work, sitting on *soft back chair*
a long period of time and with her menstrual cycle.

Pres. H. - The patient states that Dr. Wiedemeier advised that she come here for
consultation today. She states that he wants her two sets of x-rays read from a year
ago and then again in April of this year. These x-rays were taken by Dr. Joe
Krigsten for a job physical. She states that Dr. Wiedemeier wants a letter stating
whether there is any difference in the x-rays and if there is a possibility of
disability in the next ten years. She states that she has pain when doing heavy work,
such as lifting storm windows all day. She has pain if sitting on a bad chair for
a long period of time. She also has some low back pain with her menstrual cycle.
She states she has had no treatment for this other that some chiropractic treatment
for her neck. Patient is presenting at the advise of Dr. Wiedemeier.

Past H. - Appendectomy age 18; tonsillectomy age 26. No CH, GI or GU symptoms.
No allergies. Patient states she does have an ulcer.

*Says she is here only for report on the x-rays and is not here for examination
It is explained to her that if we are to send a report she will have to be
seen and examined. This is for legal purposes only.*

*Has never had treatment for her low back and states she has lost no work
because of back symptoms. States she had x-rays taken for routine job physica
a year ago and was advised at that time these must be repeated again in a year
and they were taken again in April of 1973. States she was advised by Chief
Hansen that she is to be discharged because she has potential problems
in her back. She denies any trouble with her back at anytime and has never
required treatment for her back. She works in the juvenile department
and her work consists mostly of office work and some riding in a car.*

*On examination the spine is straight, the pelvis level. Full flexion and
extension in the low back. Walks well on toes and heels. Full flexion and
extension. No lordotic curve. No lateral curve. No muscle atrophy in the
lower extremities. Good foot posture. No muscle imbalance in the legs.
Patellar reflexes are elicited on both sides, Achilles is not elicited on
either side. Babinski's are not elicited. Straight leg raising is accomplishe
to 90° bilaterally. Lasegue's test is negative bilaterally. No limitation of
motion in the hips.*

Mrs. Janell C. Rager
May 14, 1973
continued - page 2

X-rays taken by Dr. Krigsten and Grossman dated May 5, 1972 & April 3, 1973
of the lumbar spine and the dorsal spine. X-rays also taken April 3, 1973
of the cervical spine. No abnormality is seen on films of the cervical
spine. X-rays of the dorsal and lumbar spine are essentially normal.
There is noted a slight lateral curvature in the dorsal spine which I would
not expect to cause clinical problems. I see no significant abnormality
in the lumbar spine other than the mild compensatory curve.

In reviewing her history and with what information is available from
physical examination and review of x-rays, I find no disabling condition
or even potentially disabling condition in this patient.

KK/djj
cc: Dr. Wiedemeier

99

Policewoman Would Sue to Keep Her Job

An attorney for Sioux City's first policewoman has informed Police Chief William Hansen that the officer, Mrs. Janell Rager, plans to file a sex discrimination charge in U.S. District Court if necessary to resist termination of her employment.

The chief reportedly has informally notified Mrs. Rager that her service is to be terminated because of an alleged physical condition.

The Sioux City Policemen's Association reportedly decided at a meeting Thursday to support Mrs. Rager.

Chief Hansen was out of the city Friday. City Manager Wes McAllister said the matter wasn't brought to his attention until Friday and that he couldn't comment on it.

Mrs. Rager was appointed to the force in May of last year and under department procedures is still on probationary status until the end of her first year of service.

Mrs. Rager's attorney, Harry Smith, said in a letter to the chief that he has been advised that "the sole reason for her failure to achieve permanent status (with the department) is the physical problem."

According to unofficial reports, the problem involves a back condition which also showed up in a physical

Officer Janell Rager

examination before her appointment.

Policewoman Janell Rager Still on Job

Police Chief William Hansen said Friday Policewoman Janell Rager is still on the job while her future status is under discussion by her attorney and city officials.

Mrs. Rager's attorney, Harry Smith, informed Chief Hansen last week that the city's first policewoman will file a sex discrimination suit if Chief Hansen terminates her employment because of an alleged back condition.

He said Chief Hansen had advised Mrs. Rager that she would be terminated because of an X-ray report. Smith said the condition hasn't changed since an earlier X-ray taken before she was hired last May.

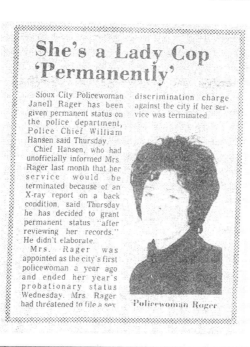

She's a Lady Cop 'Permanently'

Sioux City Policewoman Janell Rager has been given permanent status on the police department, Police Chief William Hansen said Thursday.

Chief Hansen, who had unofficially informed Mrs. Rager last month that her service would be terminated because of an X-ray report on a back condition, said Thursday he has decided to grant permanent status "after reviewing her records." He didn't elaborate.

Mrs. Rager was appointed as the city's first policewoman a year ago and ended her year's probationary status Wednesday. Mrs. Rager had threatened to file a sex discrimination charge against the city if her service was terminated.

Policewoman Rager

Juvenile Division

Working Together

Sgt. Paul Armstrong and Officer Janell Armstrong handle the in-depth interviews with nearly all rape victims in Sioux City. The married couple has worked with police officials to provide trained dispatchers and trained uniform officers on all shifts who can deal sympathetically with rape victims. They are available for informative programs about this violent crime. (Staff Photo)

Rape Defense

Report

(Editor's Note: This is the seventh in a series of articles about rape prevention and defense. The Sioux City Police Department recently has initiated a new investigation procedure for reported rapes. This is about those officers who work most closely with the victims.)

By Dianne Rose
Women's Staff Writer

It's over. Sobbing quietly, she wonders how this terrible nightmare will affect her life. What should she do? Who can she call? How will the people she loves react?

The rape victim is alone in her grief. Unlike other crimes which elicit sympathy for the victim, the woman who is raped often is made to feel like the criminal if she chooses to press charges.

A solution to this type of topsy-turvy justice is being sought by the Sioux City Police Department with a new procedure for investigations of sexual assaults.

Sgt. Paul Armstrong and his wife, Janell Armstrong, are involved in the intensive initial interview and subsequent investigation of most reported rapes.

They began working on rape cases together about a year ago. Before that, these crimes were handled by anyone in the detective bureau who happened to be available.

Often, the victim had to repeat her story many times: To the uniformed officer who answered her call, to the doctor and other hospital personnel, to the investigating team. Now she should only have to relate the minute details once.

Since every woman is a potential rape victim, it is important that every woman also understand the procedures involved immediately after the crime has been committed.

The first thing you must not do is to take a bath or shower, even though that will be your initial impulse.

Immediately head for the

102

the Sexual Assault

telephone and dial the operator or the police station. Telephone operators are trained to help in emergencies; you need only give her the information as calmly as is possible. She needs your name and the telephone number from which you are calling to help her locate you. Then give the address and describe very briefly what kind of emergency help is needed. If she asks you to stay on the line, do so; if she asks you to hang up, follow her instructions.

If you call the police station, the dispatcher will attempt to keep you on the telephone long enough to obtain specific information about the assailant in case he still is in the area and can be apprehended.

A uniformed officer who has had training in rape investigations will be dispatched to your home or your location.

He will only ask those questions necessary to write the initial report and attempt to locate the assailant. He will not ask the intimate details of the rape or assault attempt.

He also will urge that you seek medical attention and offer assistance in getting to the hospital, explaining that it is important that you do not wash or change your clothes. The physical evidence of the crime will be important if you choose to press charges.

Some victims refuse medical attention which is extremely unwise. The possibility of contracting venereal disease is very high with sexual assault. It takes some time for a woman to know whether she has V.D. and by that time it could be too late. There may already be sterility, permanent brain damage or death.

The trained officer also will inform the victim that she may wish a female relative or friend to be with her at the hospital. If the victim has no one or chooses not to call someone, he will tell her about the Rape Crisis Committee which will send a representative to be with her.

"The entire process is for the victim's comfort," Janell explained, "and also to help aid the prosecution if the case gets that far by preserving evidence."

"It is tough to get a conviction on a crime of such a serious nature which carries a maximum penalty of life in the penitentiary. We need every bit of evidence we can find," her husband added.

The examination at the hospital will take about two hours or less, depending upon how long it takes for the doctor who is on call to arrive.

The examination costs about $85, but funds will be found to help pay the cost if the victim has no money.

A policeman will not be present during this examination. If for any reason a law officer would have to be present, it would be a policewoman. It is very rare, however, that this would be necessary.

If V.D. is suspected, the doctor also probably will give you an antibiotic or penicillin.

Representatives of the police identification bureau may take pictures at the hospital of any physical injuries, which also can be used as evidence if the case comes to trial.

"Hospitals have been very cooperative in not asking rape victims a lot of questions about the crime," Janell said. "Naturally, the doctor has to ask some questions during the examination, but there is no need for the attending nurse to ask anything."

"We are trying to get away from making the victim tell her story so many times," Paul continued. "If she already has repeated the details to a uniformed officer, a nurse and a doctor, she is very irritated by the time we see her and justifiably so."

"Rape victims need to know that they will not be harrassed under the new system," Janell emphasized.

The Armstrongs normally get into the picture as soon as possible after the crime.

If the victim is exhausted and un-

willing to talk right away, she is not forced into the interview immediately.

"We have three years in which to press charges, so there is no sense to be in a hurry, but we do want the details as soon as possible in case the assailant still is in the area," Paul explained.

"It takes a load off the victim's mind usually when they find out we're married," Paul said. "Many are naturally shy and since rape is a traumatic experience, I always ask if they would rather that I leave the room. Only once that I recall has a victim requested this."

"Janell does all of the questioning usually and I just listen," he continued. "It helps to have two people listening to the story so that one may catch what the other has missed."

The Armstrongs spend as much as three to four hours with the victim explaining the procedure for prosecution so that she can decide if she wants to continue.

They must ask intimate questions about the crime such as where the assailant touched her, what he said, a description of the act, step by step, word by word, to determine if a crime actually has been committed.

National statistics indicate that about 15 per cent of reported rapes are false. Sometimes a prostitute doesn't get paid so she accuses the man of rape, sometimes a girl "eggs" a guy on, allows sexual intercourse and then changes her mind because she is worried about becoming pregnant.

The most common type of false report, however, are young girls who find themselves pregnant. They think rape is an easy explanation for their parents. Parents call the police and the investigation usually reveals the truth.

If you change your mind after you have an affair with someone; it's too late. It is not rape.

Next: A Day in Court.

Officer Janell Armstrong of the Youth Division takes careful aim at the silhouette target. These are "silencers" Officer Armstrong is wearing over her ears to soften the gunshot sounds.

Ready on the firing l

Eighty five officers of the Sioux City Police Department recently participated in the first pistol shoot of the year at James Britton Gun Range at W.

Fourth and Ivy streets.

Under the new Code of Iowa, all police officers in the state must shoot a qualifying score of 60 or above (160 is perfect) to be eligible to carry concealed weapon permits, Lt. Ronald Pettit, police training officer and pistol shoot rangemaster, said.

In addition to shooting, Pettit explained, officers also must receive a minimum of four hours in certified classroom instruction.

The top 10 shooters and their scores were Officers Rodney Clay, David Kjos, William Zellers and Milton Olsen Jr. and Lt. Pettit, 160; Officer David Hansen and Capt. Glen Hanson, 99.5, and Officers Allan Beaulaine and Rick Hamblon and Sgt. Joe Zock, 99.2.

Journal photos by Ed Porter

id Kjos, assistant rangemaster (left), yd Spaulding check the scoreboard. s assigned to the 11 p.m. to 7 a.m. i and Sgt. Spaulding works out of the vision.

Determination is the expression on the face of Lt. Michael Larsen of the Detective Division as he fires his rounds. All officers shot 50 rounds of ammunition with their service revolvers.

The Sioux City Sunday Journal, October 8, 1978—A 3

Iowa police will meet here

Some 400 Iowa police officers are expected next week in Sioux City to attend the 46th annual conference of the Iowa State Policemen's Association.

The Iowa State Policemen's Association Auxiliary also will meet.

The conclave will open Monday and will close Wednesday night. Sessions of the men's association will be at the Hilton Inn and the Oasis. The auxiliary will meet at the Hilton and the YWCA.

Capt. Ronald G. Pettit of the Sioux City Police Department is president of the ISPA. Sioux City Police Officers William Zellers and Janell Armstrong are convention cochairmen for the Sioux City Policemen's Association. Robert Bean is president of the Sioux City unit.

Monday's informal program will be a bowling tournament durinag the day at Gaylanes, advance registration, a meeting of the state executive board, a social hour and a dance, the last three events at the Hilton.

The ISPA business session will begin at 9 a. m. Wednesday at the Hilton. The Rev. William F. Skinner, pastor of the First Presbyterian Church, will give the invocation, and the city's welcome will be given by Mayor Protem Loren Callendar, City Manager Gary Pokorny, and Chief of Police Patrick Ahlstrom.

Gov. Robert Ray and Iowa Attorney General Richard C. Turner will speak at the morning meeting.

A stress seminar will be presented Tuesday afternoon by Robert Kleismet of Milwaukee and Tony Pate of Newark, N. J., who conducted a study of stress funded by the Ford Foundation for the International Conference of Police. There also will be talks by Michael Hoffman of Minneapolis, publisher of the Iowa Police Journal, and Jerry Fitzgerald of Fort Dodge, Democratic candidate for governor of Iowa.

There will be a social hour and buffet dinner Tuesday evening at the Oasis, followed by cancing to Donnie Bourett's Son Downers.

Edward Krupinsky, special agent in charge of the Federal Bureau of Investigation office at Omaha, will speak at the Wednesday morning meeting, and will introduce Special Agent Charles Wiley of Omaha, the new FBI training officer for this area. Reports will be given by Dave Killian of Fort Dodge, executive director of the Jerry Rabiner Memorial Boys Ranch, which is supported by the ISPA, and Dave Hopendorn of Des Moines, ISPA representative at the state capitol.

Officers will be elected Wednesday afternoon.

The conference will conclude with a recognition banquet Wednesday night at the Oasis. Dr. Denis Waitley, motivational psychologist of LaJolla, Calif., will be the principal speaker. Dancing at the Oasis will follow the dinner program.

Ronald Pettit   William Zellers   Janell Armstrong

Janell C. Armstrong

Stress takes its toll on police

By Bob Davis
Journal staff writer

The wife of one Sioux City police officer feels confident she can deal with the stress her husband experiences in his day-to-day contact with criminals.

After all Janelle Armstrong has been a police officer herself for over six years. She is married to Sgt. Paul Armstrong, a member of the Investigation Division. She is a member of the Crime Prevention Division.

"We're extremely understanding of one another when one of us has had a stressful day," she said.

A stressful day is not necessarily one that involves a fast car chase to catch some bad guys. It can be a day in court. Particularly if it happens to be a day off.

Robert Kleismet, a Milwaukee policeman and negotiator for the International Policemen's Association, and Tony Pate, an evaluator for the Police Foundation, say there is a high relation between the amount of time a police officer spends on court appearances and the incidents of ill health that officer suffers.

Kleismet and Pate conducted a stress seminar for the state meeting of the Iowa Policemen's Association here Tuesday.

The two men talked about a study, financed through the Ford Foundation, on how on-the-job stress effects police officers. They spoke to policemen's wives during an auxiliary meeting in the morning and to police officers at an afternoon meeting.

Kleismet said the study is a tool police associations can use in arbitration hearings. Before, he said, when associations have asked for more money because their jobs are more stressful they have lacked proof to back up those claims.

The police foundation study, he said, now can provide ammunition for those assertions.

The survey, conducted in 29 cities, showed police officers with a divorce rate of about 27 percent or over twice the national average of 13 percent of those employed in average jobs.

Pate said the divorce rate for officers married after they join the force drops to about 11 percent. The study, which included 2,200 officers, also shows a marked change in personality after an officer has been on the force three, four or five years.

In the course of study, Pate said he found that a policeman out on the street cannot always politely ask somone to leave the street or to park a car properly. Dealing with the type of people he does, a police officer frequently become angry and cynical, Pate said.

Shirley Blank, the wife of a Davenport policeman, said she can see the change in her husband on a day-to-day basis. Depending on what has happened during the day his mood can be drastically different when he comes home at night than what it was when he left for work in the morning.

Police in San Francisco, Kleismet said, are asking for the opportunity to take a year's sabbatical after every five year's of service. They argue, he said, it would give an officer a chance to renew his perspective on the world by taking another job or going to school for a year.

Lt. Loren Rubis, a Sioux City police officer, said the tension of the job caused one local patrol officer to become nauseous every morning. At first doctors thought it was psychosomatic. As it continued, doctors discovered the officer was pumping a high amount of adrenalin into his system because his job kept him wound up.

After this was discovered, Rubis said, medicine was used to return the adrenalin to a normal level.

According to the study, Pate said, departments that set rigid rules will pay for those rules through an increased incidence of traffic accidents, injuries, illnesses and divorce.

There is little that police departments and city governments can do about one interesting factor that causes stress in a police officer's life, Pate said.

The Police Foundation study, he said, shows that the greater number of children a police officer has the more likely he is to suffer fainting spells, heart attacks and to become divorced.

Cops for Christ

By Louise Zerschling
Journal staff writer

Police headquarters — where problems are the major business and officers deal with crime, trouble, dissension and woes — is seldom a place of joy and happiness, and certainly not a place of worship.

And rugged, tough police officers, seemingly cynical because they deal with the worst in human nature daily, surely aren't often envisioned as emissaries of the Lord.

Perhaps it is a miracle that is taking place within the Sioux City Police Department — there are some who would say so. Whatever it may be called, things have changed in the lives of some dozen Sioux City police officers. These officers don't have a morning coffee break. They have a morning prayer session.

They daily gather together in a second floor office at the police station, as one officer said, "to ask the Lord to bless the day and the work we are about to do, and to ask the Holy Spirit to guide us in our investigations."

It hasn't been easy. Although they were given official sanction for their own version of a coffee break, other officers and some of their friends look at them askance.

But they agree that the prayer circle has enhanced their peace, serenity and happiness, and that it has been of inestimable value in giving them the ability to deal with problems, both in their own lives and the lives of those around them.

"My bad days are better now than my good days used to be," declared Capt. Ben Bernard, a veteran policeman who heads the Crime Prevention Bureau. Bernard joined the police department in the days when to be big, tough and rugged was virtually a requirement for employment.

ence in their lives, and conclude by forming a circle with hands clasped, and giving spontaneous prayers or praise to God.

"We ask the Lord to bless our day, the other officers, and the government of our city," said Armstrong.

"The prayer meeting is not only a good thing, it's a necessity for me," said Bernard, "and if we weren't meeting here, I'd be meeting somewhere else. I do meet with other Christians throughout the week. We don't eat one meal a week and expect our body to be healthy, because you couldn't get enough food at one meal to keep our body in good condition. It's that way with spiritual food — you need a little bit now and then, and sometimes on a daily basis.

"I think people kind of get hung up on the word, 'religious.' I sometimes think there are too many 'religious' people around already. What we need are real Christians. However, I don't think that it's a case where you've got to get down on your knees and pray and throw your arms up in the air and holler. People express themselves in their own ways.

"It's not a matter of our loving God — for God loves us. Our only response is to accept his love. In the Bible Jesus said, 'I stand at the door and knock and if you open the door, I'll come in.' But the door knob is only on one side and if we don't open the door he can't come in. And again that's accepting his love, and responding to him."

Bernard said it is important to let the world know that one is a Christian.

"Can I call myself a Christian if my neighbors and friends don't know I'm a Christian?" he asked. "We can't be closet Christians. The Bible says to go out and tell the good news. And Christ told us, 'If you won't acknowledge me before men, I won't acknowledge you before like Father.'

"The problem with following Christ is

other people's lives, and in other policemen's lives. You know we have the highest divorce rate of any profession nationally, so certainly we can use some help wherever we can get it.

"When I see what the Lord's doing in other policemen's lives, I think he is doing things for people who aren't even acknowledging him. As I look back I can see some things he did in my life before I came to the point where I was ready to make a commitment to him."

"I feel a peacefulness in the division where I work at the police department, and I know the prayer meetings are a part of it," said Armstrong. "And personally, the values that experienced the entire life of my husband, Paul takes a police officer) and me have changed completely. We previously were so filled with stress — there were times Paul and I couldn't talk about our jobs for fear of not agreeing, or getting angry over justice that didn't prevail in some of the cases we were working on. We don't have any barriers any more. We know that if problems involve us personally, God fights our battles. If we didn't get the form of justice in the courts we thought it was needed in a case, we know that in the end the Lord always wins.

"I work now with those having family problems — victims of child abuse, incest, and child neglect. There are lots of time I find myself praying for those victims, and I am finding that it helps me to maintain better rapport with the victims and their families."

Another direct result of the police prayer meetings is the comparatively recent Police Chaplain Corps, an organization of Sioux City clergy. Former Chief Ahlstrom asked Bernard, because of the latter's leadership in the prayer group, to take charge of organizing such a corps, similar to one with which Ahlstrom was familiar in Colorado.

Bernard and another member of the bureau, Police Officer Janelle Armstrong, are responsible for starting the prayer meetings. Bernard is a Catholic, and Armstrong belongs to the House of Praise. None of the participants belongs to the same denomination, said Armstrong.

Bernard and Armstrong received permission from Patrick Ahlstrom, former police chief who resigned recently to return to Colorado, to use their morning coffee break for the prayer meeting.

Every weekday morning at about 8 a.m., from five to a dozen police officers and a civilian employe or two meet for about 10 to 15 minutes in Bernard's office. There they give testimony, if they feel like doing so, about Christ's influ-

that we're always concerned with what the world thinks of us, and what friends say, like 'My God, I keep following Christ is a good thing, but why not keep it quiet? What will your friends think?'

"Every time I make a recommitment to Christ, I know I'm right, that's all. I've turned the door knob. I can't be concerned with what the world thinks. At least if I'm not so concerned, I'm on the right track."

And have the prayer meetings had results?

The participants respond with a resounding "Yes."

Policemen may deal with society's problems, but they also have problems of their own, said Bernard.

"I see evidence of Christ's work in

The corps was formed in charge of Sioux City Catholic, Protestant (including Evangelical), and minorities ministries. The more than 30 clergy volunteers have 24-hour assignments on rotation, and are on call for the police in the cases of bad accidents, rape, murder, or any case where a chaplain's help is needed.

The steering committee is composed of Capt. Bernard, the Rev. Sara Speer, assistant pastor at the First Presbyterian Church; the Rev. Don Rowian of the Morningside Assembly of God; the Rev. Don Lachman of the First Covenant Church; the Rev. Louis Kollasch of the Cathedral of the Epiphany, and the Rev. Bill Pace of the ministries division of Siouxland Metro Ministries.

Police Lt. Michael Larson carries a revolver and a badge, and his lapel bears a pin showing his religious commitment. (Journal photos by Bob Davis)

Service club honors three police officers

Three police officers have been honored for excellence in their profession by a city service club.

Sgt. Boyd Spaulding, a 26-year-veteran of the department, has been named policeman of the year. The club annually bestows the honor, selecting an officer from nominees supplied by the department.

Departing from tradition, the club chose this year to honor a husband and wife team on the force, Sgt. Paul Armstrong and Officer Janell Armstrong. They were named police persons of the year by the Exchange Club.

Spaulding has been a sergeant since 1978. He has worked in most of the divisions of the department. He was one of the organizers of the K-9 patrol and was the dog training officer for 16 years, beginning in 1961.

A two-year Navy veteran, Spaulding also has been cited numerous times by the department. He also has taken many training courses offered by the department.

He has been cited as a "sincere, dedicated, accommodating police officer."

Paul Armstrong, 38, joined the force in 1963, receiving a promotion to his present rank in 1971.

He has served 4½ years in the youth bureau, 7 years as an investigator and 5½ years on the uniformed shift. Armstrong currently serves with the 7-3 uniform shift.

Janell Armstrong, 38, became an officer in 1972. She served seven years with the youth bureau and is currently assigned to the investigative division.

The Armstrongs have been credited with aiding hundreds of wayward juveniles during the years.

They've counseled and helped change many attitudes of kids in trouble, according to the Exchange Club citation. The couple worked with the rape crisis committee when it was formed and at the time investigated all reported rape cases.

The couple is also active in the House of Praise.

Police will recruit women, minorities

By Bob Gunsolley
Journal staff writer

The city employee relations department is starting what is believed to be the first concerted effort to encourage minorities and women to apply for positions in the Sioux City police department.

The department has five vacancies which it won't be able to fill until another eligibility list is created, probably this fall. The first step is a recruiting campaign officially starting Monday.

The application period is from Monday to July 11. Applications may be obtained in room 100 at City Hall.

The Police-Citizens Advisory Committee recently urged a greater effort to get more minorities and women in the department and created an ad hoc committee to work out such an effort with Sandra Trevathan, the city's administrative assistant for equal employment opportunity.

The police department now has three minority members and one woman. Although the three minority members in a total force of 113 represent about the same proportion as minorities in the local population, no new minority members have been added to the force since 1975, she said.

Trevathan would like to establish a goal for women, who, she said, should be much better represented on the police force even though it is a non-traditional role for them. First, she said, she wants to complete an affirmative action analysis for the entire city workforce.

The recruiting campaign will include appearances by various officials before appropriate organizations to encourage applications by minorities and women, public service announcements, perhaps some neighborhood recruiting by present officers and advertisements in both local and out-of-town papers.

Among cities to carry the ads will be Omaha, Des Moines, Davenport and Waterloo.

Janelle Armstrong, the only woman on the force, will make some of the recruiting appearances.

The ads will state the beginning salary and qualifications. They will be aimed at qualified men and women, with special encouragement to minorities and women.

Human rights groups in the this region also will be enlisted in helping to spread the word, Trevathan said.

The goal is to get enough applications to produce an eligibility list of 10 candidates and a second backup list after completion of examinations during the summer. The last examination period produced only 10 people out of 100 who took out applications.

A lot drop out along the way as they go through a fairly rigid schedule of written and oral examinations, physical examinations and physical agility tests. The Civil Service Commission recently made it easier by revising the examination schedule to reduce the number of steps from four to three.

For those who might be interested, the starting bi-weekly salary for a police officer is $554.90, or $14,482 annually.

Applicants must be able to read and write the English language, be

CHRISTIAN PROFILE: A POLICE WOMAN

by Cathee Phillips

"He can bring me up. I don't have to struggle and climb the rope all by myself." Janell Armstrong says these words with conviction. They have been proven real in her own life.

Eleven years ago, Janell's life began to change. Desiring a challenge in her life, she chose to become a policewoman and was hired to work with juveniles by the Sioux City Police Department.

As a single, working mother, her life was not easy. One constant worry was the atmosphere of the neighborhood school which her children attended. Encouraged by her fellow police officers to take her children out of this school, she then admitted them to a Catholic school — never dreaming how this would change her life.

A teacher, Sister Evelyn, visited Janell. Over the next year, they became close friends. Sister Evelyn

would babysit Janell's children, or Janell would lend her the car. All this time, she accepted Janell as she was and never said a word about her drinking or her life style. Many of the Sister's friends would ask her why she was wasting her time on Janell, who was "hopeless". The Sister continued to "waste her time".

During one of their many phone conversations, Janell was upset over a personal problem. For the first

time, the Sister offered advice, "Take a look at where your life is at. Have you ever sat down and prayed about it?"

Startled, Janell decided to follow the suggestion, and God responded to her prayer with an immediate solution to her problem.

"In Christianity," Janell shares, "some are seekers and some are found. They seek the Lord or the Lord finds them. At that time, i became a seeker."

It was a three year process before Janell felt truly committed to Christ. And it was at a "cursillo" (a week-end retreat sponsored by the Catholic church) she found a dedication beyond experience.

During the time of seeking, she met and married her husband, Paul Armstrong, who also found faith in Christ during a Lutheran sponsored cursillo. Paul is a day uniform sergeant on the Sioux City Police Force.

Janell presently serves in the Crime Prevention Division which oversees the school fingerprinting programs, home security, etc. Her

commitment to Christ has made a definite impact on her career.

Once, while working with juveniles, she had to talk to a lady about her runaway son. Janell tried to be as helpful and kind as she could. About three weeks later, while on a call, Janell twisted her ankle and fell down in the middle of the street. Her radio went flying beyond her reach. Suddenly, this same lady came out from a house and into the middle of the street. She helped Janell up, gave her the radio, helped her to the car, and left without a word.

"People like her just don't help police officers like that," Janell states. "But, because of my kindness to her, God returned it to me as a blessing."

About two years ago, Paul and Janell received the Police Officers of the Year Award. The assistant chief shared with them that their Christian attitudes helped to change a negative atmosphere in their divisions in a more positive one. Many people tell Janell—"hey, you've really got it all together!" And it does seem so. Energetic and

optimistic, Janell somehow finds time to help out at cursillos, teach aerobics at her church, sew like crazy and run five times a week as well as be a wife, mother and policewoman. She has six children who she lovingly refers to as "Yours, Mine and Ours": Greg, 21 and Glen, 19, who both work at HyVee and Shirley, 6; LuAnn, married and living in Sioux City; Brad, 23, who works at Sunshine; and Don, 20, a carpenter. She also has three grandchildren to keep her busy.

"But," Janell explains, "I don't really have it all together. I feel that there's a common misconception that it isn't an everyday struggle when you're a Christian. Every day when I falter, I have to call on Jesus. I just can't do it without Him. Christians struggle—we think **we** can do it—but, we need Jesus. I need to be myself—to be accepted—faults and all. We need to accept others as they are. Sister Evelyn accepted me as I was; she wasted her time. Look what it did for me."

Janell, He has truly brought you up in life. Hey—maybe you **do** have it all together.

February 8, 1984

Chief Gerald P. Donovan
Asst. Chief Robert Worden

This is a written grievance, in accord with the
procedure, after having been notified through
the Chain of Command verbally on February 6, 1984,
that my request reference my senority issue has been refused.
The request is that my senority as a Police Officer be
made effective as of the date of my hire, May 15, 1972.

Officer Janell C. Armstrong
Officer Janell C. Armstrong

2/9/84

This grievance relates to Article XII, Section 12.01,
12.02, and 12.03 of Agreement Between City of Sioux
and The Sioux City Policemen's Association.

Officer Janell C. Armstrong
Officer Janell C. Armstrong

POLICE DEPARTMENT
SIOUX CITY, IOWA

Date: February 10, 1984   Department Memorandum

To: Officer Janell Armstrong   No. ___84-4___

Subject: Denial of Grievance

I have received your grievance dated February 8, 1984 relating
to Article XII, Sections 12.01, 12.02 and 12.03 of the contract
between the City of Sioux City and the Sioux City Policemen's
Association.

I am denying your grievance for the following reason:

Article XII, Sections 12.01, 12.02 and 12.03 refer to
Police Officer. Your status was that of Police Woman
until August 28, 1976, at that time your position was
described as Police Officer.

This position and rank in seniority have been listed
on the Police Department's seniority list, as submitted
to us by Donnabelle Benson, Clerk for the Civil Service
Commission, every year.

GERALD P. DONOVAN
Chief of Police

GPD:bn

cc: Employee Relations Department

SCPD Form 6
Rev. 2/83

112

LAW OFFICES

SMITH & SMITH

632-645 BADGEROW BLDG.
SIOUX CITY, IOWA 51101
TELEPHONE (712) 255-8094

HARRY H. SMITH
MacDONALD SMITH
LeROY J. STURGEON
DENNIS M. McELWAIN

SOUTH DAKOTA OFFICE
ROBERT O'CONNOR, RESIDENT ATTORNEY
827 West Sixth St.
Sioux Fals, South Dakota 57102-0579
Telephone (605) 336-1088

February 15, 1984

Mr. J. R. Castner, City Manager
101 City Hall
Sioux City, IA 51101

Dear Mr. Castner:

Re: Janell Armstrong Grievance
Police Department No. 84-4

Pursuant to Article X, Section 10.4, this is to advise you Ms. Armstrong appeals the subject grievance to you per Step 4 of the grievance procedure. Attached is a copy of Chief Donovan's answer of February 10, 1984.

As you know, this grievance may also involve corrective action by the civil service commission. Accordingly, we have no problem with your delaying hearing at your step for a reasonable time to allow the parties to determine the proper role of the commission in this matter.

Thank you.

Respectfully,

MacDonald Smith

MS/ck

cc: Janell Armstrong
    Pete Groetken
    Phil Murphy
    Gerald P. Donovan

TO: Gerald P. Donovan, Chief of Police

FROM: Janell Armstrong

DATE: February 15, 1984

SUBJECT: Possible Transfer to Uniform Shift

      Assistant Chief Worden recently advised me that I would be transferred to the 3-11 uniform shift commencing April 1, 1984. He further suggested that I submit to you a written statement of my shift preference. I am, therefore, writing this letter pursuant to his suggestion. I do want to make it clear I am not and have not requested a transfer. I am writing this only to setout my shift preference in the event I am transferred.

      My preferences for a shift in the uniform division are in the following order:

          (1)   Watch I
          (2)   Watch III
          (3)   Watch II

My preferences are based on the fact I have a seven year old daughter. Either Watch I or Watch III will permit me to spend necessary time with her while I am off duty. Watch II will result in my having no time with her on a regular daily basis, since she is going to school.

      Respectfully,

      Janell Armstrong

cc: Assistant Chief Worden
    Pete Groetken

February 22, 1984

Mr. MacDonald Smith
Attorney
632-640 Badgerow Bldg.
Sioux City, IA 51101

Dear Mr. Smith:

I have had the opportunity to review the material filed pertaining to the
Janelle Armstrong grievance. It is my contention that this is a matter for
determination by the Civil Service Commission, and as such it is not grievable
under the labor agreement. Therefore I do not plan to conduct a hearing on this
grievance at my level now or in the future.

Sincerely,

J. R. Casner
City Manager

sn/22/c

cc: Phil Murphy, Employee Relations Director
     Janelle Armstrong
     Pete Groetken, President
     Police Association
     Jim Daley, Assistant City Attorney
     Gerald Donovan, Police Chief

OFFICE OF CITY MANAGER
101 CITY HALL
P.O. BOX 447
SIOUX CITY, IOWA 51102
(712) 279-6302

115

Horse mutilation work of predators

from page one

were looking for answers. I told them, "When you see strange happenings, report them to your school liaison officer, to your parents, to the sheriff's department, or to the youth director at the church, immediately."

Floss said the speaker talked for 20 minutes, then asked for questions. "I would say the questions came from the comments she made, for the most part. Our purpose in scheduling the discussion was to help make our stu-dents aware of cultism and Satan worship," Floss said.

The woman later said of those caught up in Satan worship, "When they go from high school to college or to work, their interest in Satanism fades."

One law enforcement officer be-lieves that, during her church group visit, the rumor about the pending sacrifice of a blue-eyed blonde girl was started anew, only this time it was to be on the winter solstice, Dec. 22.

It didn't happen.

Sheriff's Deputy Dave Kjos says, "Satan worship does not call for female sacrifices ... Furthermore, Dec. 22 is a feast day, not a sacrifice day."

• Item — In September, the Woodbury County Sheriff's Depart-ment investigates complaints of animal mutilation in the Hornick area (lots of Loess Hills, remote wooded areas). A dead horse is found in an advanced state of decomposi-tion, its genitalia missing.

A veterinarian called as a consul-tant believes the missing parts have been chewed away by small predators rather than cut off with a knife, says Kjos.

Experienced hunters and trappers echo the veterinarian's belief. Small predators, such as coyotes or feral dogs, seek not only the obvious free meal but also remove the genitalia to get at tender internal organs.

Says Sheriff's Capt. Dave Amick, a hunter since boyhood, "I grew up on the farm. I've seen many animals which have been mutilated by other animals. You can tell whether they have been cut with a knife or chewed. Small animals eat the tender tissue first and gain access to the body cavi-ty that way."

Says Kjos, "We have nothing con-crete about Satan worship or cults at East High School. Most of what we hear is rumors."

2—The Sioux City Journal, Sunday, April 12, 1987

ublic sees new police/fire building

ce Officer Janell Armstrong explains to visitors how the com-er system works during open house and a tour Saturday of

Sioux City's new police/fire headquarters building (Staff pho by Gary Anderson)

117

Janell C. Armstrong

Skinned deer triggers more rumors

By Harvey M. Sanford
Journal staff writer

Tuesday night during an East-at-West High School basketball game the frozen carcass of a skinned, dressed-out deer was placed atop a car in the host school's north parking lot.

In addition to being skinned and gutted, the deer's feet and head had been removed.

The discovery ballooned into a rash of rumors linking the act with Satan worship. By the time the animal carcass was removed from the parking lot Thursday morning, elements of

the rumor were that:
• The act was a threat from the cult to the driver of the car.
• The driver of the car was a blue-eyed blonde girl.

Wayne Buchholtz, Stone State Park attendant who removed the animal from a snowbank at the north edge of the parking lot Thursday, Conservation Officer Steve Jauron of Sergeant Bluff and West High School Liaison Officer Rick Saunders pooled their observations of the animal.

They said it was thoroughly frozen, that it appeared to have been field-dressed and that the meat was of sufficient age to indicate the deer had been killed during the legal hunting season.

Said Saunders, "I believe some kids saw this carcass hanging somewhere and decided to toss it on top of some car as a prank. I think they picked the car because it was one of the best looking ones in the lot."

The 1982 sports car was driven by a 17-year-old senior from East High School.

"I didn't touch it," she said of the deer. She reported it to school authorities and Saunders followed up.

He said, "I asked her if she had any enemies. She said she knew of none. I asked specifically if she was a member of a cult. She said she was not. She could think of no reason why

someone would single her out for incident."

More than that, the East senior is a brunette, not a blue-blonde.

Last fall, before Halloween, rumor circulated like wildfire in Morningside community that a b eyed blonde girl was to be sacrif by a cult of Satan worshippers.

It didn't happen.

But the unsubstantiated rumor given such such mouth-to-mouth petus that a number of East

SEE BLACK
continued on page A8

Black attire has no link to Satanism

from page one

School students were genuinely frightened, and their understandably protective parents were besieging East High School officials and law enforcement officers with demands that they do something.

That something included cracking down on a number of girls who dressed in black and who were rumored to be witches.

• East High School Principal Jim Deignan said Thursday he had called the girls who dressed in black into his office, and their parents as well, and he found they were hurt by the rumors.

"When you watch them all crying, it bothers you," said Deignan. "They (the girls in black) are not disruptive in school. They are good students, good citizens. Just because they choose to dress differently is really no cause to call them witches.

"If you're really not concerned that what you say might hurt a person, it is really sad. The one thing I am sure of is that the persons who took part in these rumors, which have no basis in fact, have really hurt teachers and students, and hurt them badly," Deignan said.

Two of the girls who dress in black made unsolicited calls to The Journal to say they were grateful for Thursday's story, and hoped the rumors would come to an end. They reaffirmed they were not witches, but simply liked to dress differently from the rest of their schoolmates.

• There was another rumor before Halloween that the same cult was going to harm children as they went out to "trick or treat."

That caused several parents at Immaculate Conception Elementary School to express concern to the school principal, Sister Kathy Avery. She made inquiries and then included the following paragraph in the November issue of Immaculate Conception's note to parents:

"We have had some reports that cults are threatening to do harmful things on Halloween. After checking with Janelle Armstrong, police liaison officer, we have found that this (the rumor) is true. She encourages you to go with your children if they go out on Halloween. No child should be on their own, even at the malls. Take extra precautions."

Halloween came and went without reports of harm to children trick or treating.

• One rumor is that there are cult practitioners in other city schools.

Says Richard B. Lilly, West High School principal: "As far as I know, we have had no problems with cults or rumors of cults. We heard from another school a rumor that there was a cult member here, but I have found none."

Says Paul VanderWiel, North High School principal: "I don't know if we have such a thing. We do have some kids who dress in black, but we have no cult rumors. Nothing has come back to us from faculty, counselors or the liaison officer."

Says Dorene Red Cloud, North High student: "My sister and I like to dress in black, but we are not witches. We believe in being ourselves, in doing our own thing. Those rumors hurt."

Says the Rev. Victor Ramaeker, superintendent of Heelan High School, on whether there are cult followers at his school: "I heard a parent raise the question a few days ago, and that is the first I have heard about it."

Says Conrad Cameron, principal of East Middle School: "I have heard nothing whatsoever. I have not even heard the term 'cult' discussed in the hallways, the lunchroom or wherever."

118

Door to door evacuation efforts, 1990 flood waters.

Janell C. Armstrong

Janell Armstrong has been with the Sioux City Police Department for nearly 15 years.

Today's Woman

Policewoman enjoys job

After nearly 18 years on the Sioux City Police Force, Janell Armstrong, 48, remarks, "I can't ever say that it has not been interesting."

When Janell joined the police force in 1972 she worked in the juvenile division as an investigator. She was also the first woman police officer.

Her duties have changed several times since that time. After five or six years of working with juveniles, she worked on adult investigations for three more years. Janell was then moved into crime prevention for two years.

In 1984 Janell got her first taste of patrol duty as she worked on Watch III, patrolling nights for three years.

She says, "I recently came out of the liaison position. I was the East High liaison officer for three years and I just hated to give it up."

Currently, Janell is working Watch I which is patrolling the streets from 6:30 a.m. to 2:30 p.m.

"We start with roll call in the morning and get assigned a district. With that district assignment, you get occasional checks you make, radar checks that citizens want to have made and you do those in between answering calls that the dispatcher sends you on." She adds, "In between that, you work traffic."

When working day hours, she receives several calls regarding traffic accidents, abandoned vehicles, and burglaries that occurred the night before and were discovered the following morning. There are also early morning alarm calls — people will go to work and will forget to turn off the alarm. This often leads to several false alarms, however

sometimes they are legitimate.

She finds contact with people to be the most enjoyable part of the job. Janell says she makes a point of stopping and talking to people. Although Janell likes the contact with people that patrolling brings, her first love as a police officer is working with juveniles.

"There are two things that I have done that I really enjoy. Number one is working with the juveniles and then in adult investigations. I was involved in a majority of investigations of sexual assault. I really enjoyed that. I feel that those cases take patience and compassion," she explains. "It takes a lot of nurturing to get victims through that investigation."

At the time she first applied for the police department, Janell had been an executive secretary. It was her strong desire to work with juveniles that encouraged her to apply for the position as a juvenile investigator.

"I initially wanted to work with the youth because I had youth of my own that I was raising, and I think because I struggled as a youth myself. I felt like sometimes kids were looked at as troublesome instead of as a blessing." She continued to say, "I am not sure what starts kids on trouble; I think there are varied factors. But I know that no matter what caliber they are, they respond if you care about them."

In addition to having contact with the general public, Janell says the care and concern among the troops is another enjoyable factor in her job.

When Janell is not keeping busy patrolling the streets, she fills her time with gardening, sewing and is active in church work. She also teaches aerobics which has currently disbanded for summer.

121

Janell with the Crash Dummies

Speech Class Welcomes Guest Speaker

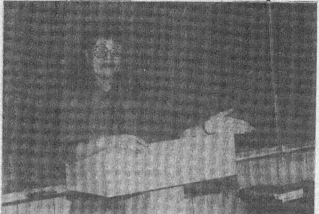

Exciting, action-packed, and dangerous are some of the terms one could use to describe Janell Armstrong's career as a police woman with the Sioux City Police Department.

Mrs. Armstrong took time from her busy schedule to speak to several speech and English classes last Friday. Through many interesting stories, she told how she came to be the first woman police officer in Sioux City. She re-lived her first few years on the police squad, and described to the students the fear and rejection she faced as a victim of discrimination.

Nonetheless, Officer Armstrong persevered and worked to become the best policewoman she could be. She certainly wouldn't have lasted twenty-two years on the police force if she had given up!

Mrs. Armstrong stated that she preferred the night shift because that shift is action-filled and the officers are always busy, "If I had a choice, that would be the shift I'd work, but my family, on the other hand, might object."

A great many changes have occurred since she first began working on the force. Women today are given approximately the same training as men, but when Armstrong started, she was given little combat training and knew only a little about the weapons which police officers used. Today, she practices shooting each month and is evaluated on her shooting ability each quarter.

Armstrong started working inside, but eventually she was placed on the street with the men. She said this was quite difficult, because she was totally unprepared for street work. She said the officers she worked with were very helpful and gave her numerous pointers which probably saved her life.

After twenty-two years on the force, Armstrong has come to the conclusion that women should not be given the same duties as the men on the force. Women are not as strong as men, and they have different skills--physically and psychologically--she stated.

Armstrong witnessed to her Christian faith, and stated that an important part of her day is time spent in prayer. She commented that before she reaches the scene of a call, she prays.

Armstrong plans to retire in three years. She has made a great contribution to the Sioux City Police Force. She will be missed.

Women of Excellence receive recognition

Six Siouxland women were honored for their leadership, strength of character and accomplishments Tuesday night during the Women of Excellence recognition banquet.

Louise Zerschling, Nina Anderson, Janell Armstrong, Virginia Bitterly, Margaret Sanders and Shelly Archer were selected from a field of 23 nominees.

The 13th annual ceremony was held at the Sioux City Convention Center to honor the contributions made by women. The event is sponsored by Women Aware, an agency that helps displaced homemakers and women.

The candidate were sponsored by service clubs, businesses, churches and individuals. The women were nominated in six categories.

Zerschling, Sioux City, was honored in the category of "Women Pursuing Truth." She was nominated by Quota International of Sioux City.

Zerschling, "Out of the Past" columnist and retired staff member of the Sioux City Journal, was recognized for being a pioneer in journalism who has been an advocate for excellence in reporting and editing. She was the first woman in every position she undertook at the newspaper. She has been involved in a variety of community activities, worked on freedom of information issues and encouraged young women to pursue nontraditional careers.

Anderson, Lawton, Iowa, was recognized in the category of "Women Striving to Improve the Quality of Life." She was nominated by the Near Northside Neighborhood Coalition.

Anderson was a catalyst in helping to form the neighborhood group in 1991 to do something about crime and safety in the area around 12th and Douglas streets. As a member of St. Thomas Episcopal Church, Anderson got the congregation involved in the coalition. She was instrumental in raising funds to create two "pocket parks," started a summer program for children and volunteered for many programs at her church.

Zerschling   Anderson

Armstrong   Bitterly

Sanders   Archer

Armstrong, Sioux City, was honored in the category of "Women Taking Risks." She was nominated by the Sioux City Police Department.

Armstrong, who recently retired after 25 years as a police officer, was credited with opening the doors for other women in law enforcement, a profession that has been primarily male dominated. She was the first woman officer certified by the state on the department. As an officer, she was compassionate and dedicated to helping people, setting a high standard for all officers to follow.

Bitterly, Le Mars, Iowa, was honored in the category of "Women Working Creatively." She was nominated by Dixie Feuerstein.

She was credited with 36 years of volunteering, ranging from the young to the elderly. She established the "Lifeline" health care services in Plymouth County, encouraged 2,000 4-H volunteers and promoted volunteer workshops. She nurtured the growth of young piano students and visits nursing home residents where she often uses music therapy.

Sanders, Sioux City, was recognized in the category of "Women Helping Women." She was nominated by the staff and volunteers of the Council of Sexual Assault and Domestic Violence (CSADV).

Sanders was credited with providing stable and visionary leadership as executive director of CSADV, a position she accepted in 1990. Because of her planning, the agency raised $850,000 and constructed a new shelter to help women and children escape violence. She established a number of programs, fostered personal growth for women in need and served as a role model and mentor for her staff.

Archer, Sergeant Bluff, was honored in the category of "Young Women of Excellence." She was nominated by her husband, Kevin Archer.

Archer is a wife, mother of two small children and a small business owner. In November 1995, the Archers purchased a franchise called Surface Doctor, when she was seven months pregnant. She left a part-time job to work full time in the business, while juggling being a homemaker and carrying for two children. She was recognized for being a role model for young women.

The recipients were selected by a panel of judges. Charlotte Nelson, executive director of the Iowa Commission on the Status of Women, was the keynote speaker. Denny Bullock, general sales manager of KSCJ/KSUX, was the master of ceremonies.

TWELVE

And The Prejudice Rises to the Surface

Romans 5: 3-5—Not only so, but we also rejoice in our sufferings, because we know that suffering produces perseverance; perseverance, character; and character, hope. And hope does not disappoint us, because God has poured out his love into our hearts by the Holy Spirit, whom he has given us. (NIV)

In January 1979 I was transferred to the General Investigations Division as the Juvenile and Child Abuse Division had been abolished during a restructuring of the entire department.

I worked for one Captain in the division who was then transferred elsewhere and I was then under the command of someone that I shall refer to as Captain Nasty.

The first day he took over, he accused me of being late for roll call and made a complete spectacle in front of the entire group of detectives. I wish I could project to you the height of the humiliation that I felt while He spoke to me in this manner. I would have preferred being hung by my toes in the town square (if we had one).

I say this humorously but the emotion started to swell in my innermost being. It was very small at first and gradually became larger and larger. I can best describe it by using the words I heard at a class I attended. I was slowly feeling like a "wrong, bad" person.

He made several comments from the podium directed at me. "You may have gotten what you wanted up until this point, but now things are going to be different." And, "Now you are going to work for a change."

Never were these comments directed at me individually but always in the presence of the entire Detective Division. I had never worked for this man nor did I even know him except by appearance. I remained silent and another detective pointed out that it was now 8:45 and that roll call had always started at 8:50.

Mature supervisors would have apologized at this point but Captain Nasty suddenly turned mute. From that moment until my departure from Investigations, my work was continually criticized and even the impossible expected to be made possible.

One area in law enforcement that most officers did not want any part of was the responsibility of talking to community organizational groups. Shortly after being assigned to the unit, I was asked to help out with an investigation. There had been many house burglaries in one area of the city.

One of the homeowners had been contacted at his place of business and asked by the caller if the homeowner would like to buy his stuff back. The homeowner was jubilant as some of the items taken were sentimental as well as valuable. The homeowner contacted the investigators and relayed the information.

A sting type operation was set up. Several officers and I would appear to be working in the homeowner's business and be present when the burglar came to "sell" back the owner's belongings. The operation was successful and a couple of arrests were made.

The following day, I had been asked to give a presentation to an organizational group regarding the workings of the department. After delivering my talk, I allowed for a time of questions and answers.

The scenario mentioned above about the arrest of the burglars had been front-page news that particular morning. It had also been reported that a judge had allowed the men to sign their own bonds and they had been released from incarceration.

Needless to say, the headline story was brought up and numerous questions were asked about the arrests, the perpetrators, and last but by all means not least about the Judge who had granted them to sign their own bonds. I answered the questions by utilizing policy procedures and avoided references to this particular case. I explained that any reference to specifics would not be appropriate, as the case had not gone to court and the investigation still had not been closed.

One of the questions posed to me was, "Is there anything that we can do when we read continually in the paper that a specific judge has been, in our opinion, too lenient?"

I answered by talking about court watchers who monitored courtrooms, listening to evidence and worked as advocates to crime victims. I also responded by telling the listeners that everyone has the opportunity at their voting booths to reject judges by voting not to retain them.

Upon returning to the station, Captain Nasty immediately summoned me to his office and abruptly told me to close the door. He demanded that I sit and he very loudly asked me, "What in the hell did you think you were doing this afternoon?"

I had absolutely no idea what he was talking about so naturally I asked him.

He retorted, "You know exactly what I am referring to. I received a phone call from Judge Gobal right after you left the community center. He was livid about your condemning him and stating that he was derelict in his duty."

I tried several times to inject the truth into this tirade and I was told to sit there and shut up.

After he became hoarse from yelling at me, he concluded by saying, "I am demanding that you leave here, go straight to Judge Gobal and apologize for your ignorance. You will be most fortunate if he does not make a formal complaint against you."

I replied by saying, "Captain, Judge Gobal was not at that gathering and I have no idea what someone told him, but I did not in anyway refer to him, or this case. My references were in general without condemnation toward anyone. Therefore, I shall not be apologizing to anyone. So suspend me however many days you desire as I will not be visiting the Judge."

He dismissed me and it was not mentioned again.

For three years I worked under these conditions, thinking that God had abandoned me. Our prayer group had been disbanded due to retirements and members being transferred to other shifts, etc. However, I had established a foundation of prayer at that place of employment and I did not start a day without asking God to be at the center of it. Good thing or I would have probably taken things into my own hands a few times.

Harsh conditions develop prayer lives and give us a great deal of time to learn perseverance. Only God knows the necessary time span and the amount of adversity needed to improve our Christ-like character. Mine must have lacked a lot.

One beautiful sunshiny day a female news reporter from one of the television channels contacted me and requested that I assist her on a week long daily series on "Women in Blue."

My role was to be interviewed by this stunning reporter as I described women in uniform police work. I politely refused her offer for this part in her nightly television series. She called me two or three additional times in an attempt to coerce me to do the interview. "For the betterment of the department", she said.

Each time she called, I returned her call and nicely informed her machine that I did not have any intention of being a part of her interview as I did not work in blue and I thought she was asking someone who did not have all the facts.

The reporter's request was based upon the fact that the department had hired a female who was attending the police academy with intention upon her graduation to put her in uniform. Personally, I had not worked in uniform and I felt that a weeklong series would be a lot of unneeded pressure on this candidate, not to mention the fact that I did not have the experience required to properly respond to the interview.

Part two of this story, the Chief of Police called me to his office and told me that a certain television reporter had contacted him and related that I had been rude to her. I said to the Chief, "If the definition of rude is the fact that I denied her an interview then I was rude to her."

The Chief said, "I would like you to do this interview."

My response was, "If I am being ordered to be a part of this series then I will do so."

The Chief's retort went like this: "I am not ordering you to do this. I just don't understand why you don't want to represent our department."

In an attempt to make my feelings understood, I replied, "I believe that I would be laughed out of this department if I participate in this television series and make it appear to the public as though I have been a uniform police officer, when, for the past twelve years, everyone here, and every agency that we work with knows that I have been a plainclothes officer."

With that I was dismissed and told that he was not making it mandatory. I did not do the interview. The young lady who was attending the Police Academy did not complete the course and thus we did not have a new uniform policewoman after all.

Three or four weeks passed and I exhaled a sigh of relief believing that the journalist issue had passed. And, indeed, that particular reporter incident had passed by the wayside. However, the city had an Equal Employee Opportunity Officer who called me asking that I appear with her on a television spot to encourage female participation in my career. My heart plunged toward my toenails as I declared, "I'd rather not."

By the end of the shift, I received the summons to visit with the Chief. My first facetious thought was "How kind of him to invite me." My mind immediately went to "The first request was not heeded but this one will or he'll know the reason why."

BINGO—I couldn't have been more right. I voiced my opinion, he voiced his and in the twinkling of an eye, I was visiting the EEO Officer. She smugly met with me and ordered me to accompany her at the television studio in uniform.

Smugly I retorted, "I have not *ever* had a uniform as I have always worked plainclothes positions."

Miss or Mista EEO Officer then told me to meet her dressed looking more like a man. She suggested that I read a book entitled "How Women Should Dress for Success." I waltzed through the television segment and maintained a great attitude albeit that I wore my normal clothing.

Time just flies when you're having fun, and two or three long weeks sailed by before my Sergeant advised me that I was to go to the Assistant Chief's office. I was a smidgeon insulted that I had been handed off to the second in command.

With great reluctance and panic type anticipation, I pretended as though I was in total control of my emotional stability and I strolled into his office—after being announced.

This meeting was short, sweet and to the point. Indeed it was short, rather sour and there was no point only a "gotcha" point. Chief David, I was told, had made the decision to transfer me to the uniform shift starting April 1. The words that he said entered my ears as, "There are three shifts, you have a choice between Watch II; 2:30 PM to 10:30PM or Watch III; 10:30 PM to 6:30 AM."

Feigning calmness I asked, "May I have a day to review the options with my family?"

He quickly replied, "Request granted."

As I was dismissed, I was handed a copy of the police department's current seniority list. I gripped this document in my hand without even studying it. I would review it when I arrived home.

At home, in the comfort of privacy, I tried to make sense of this action. I wept. I ranted. I raved. I threatened to quit. Brandon then encouraged me to quit with these words, "Our daughter is nine years old, if you work Watch II and I work Watch I we will never see each other."

As glorious as quitting sounded, I had already put in eleven years and eleven months. That time frame was not going to provide me a very lucrative pension. Swiftly with tongue in cheek, I offered the possibility of working 10:30 PM to 6:30 AM—Watch III.

Keep in mind here that I had long ago given up the nightlife and 10 PM is just slightly beyond my bedtime. This produced some wrinkles to be ironed out, but we concluded that we could manage this on the home front.

Remember the seniority list I had gripped in my paw as I left the Assistant Chief's office? Prior to transferring to uniform, I had never seen this list. Imagine my surprise when I see that I am listed as having six years, nine months and two days service. In real life, I had eleven years and eleven months on the job. While working plainclothes seniority did not have much significance. In uniform, seniority has tremendous value. Vacations, of course, are determined by seniority. Squad cars were allocated by number of year's service. Undesirable tasks are even distributed to those lagging on the list. There were approximately eleven or twelve individuals listed ahead of me on the official list who actually were hired anywhere from 6 months to 4 years after me.

Now honestly, I'm tired of fighting but on the other hand, I have no intention of sitting on my laurels after being relieved of approximately 5 years of duty.

I made an appointment to talk with my Sergeant, my Lieutenant, my Captain, the Assistant Chief and the Chief. That is the Chain of command—you know. The top of the chain informed me, "The first 6 years, 9 months and 2 days service I was classified as a Police Woman. My classification was then changed to Police Officer."

See Pages 111 – 115

Let me think. I'm still a woman and I'm still with the police and I'm still an Officer. What have I missed here? The fact was that no reference was ever made to me that any restructuring was done not to mention that *my* position and title had been revised.

In order to rectify this, Chief David informed me that I must verbally file a grievance, which I did, on the spot. Next step, as he equally as fast denied my verbal grievance, was to submit a written grievance. He in turn denied it.

Next step—written grievance to the City Manager. He denied it with the explanation that to make or change seniority status requires action by the Civil Service Commission. Thus, I now needed to file a complaint with the Civil Service Commission. I had no clue what the procedure might be or the paperwork necessary to prove my position with the Civil Service Commission. Of one thing I was positive—the Civil Service Commission did not change my classification.

As always, when backed into a corner, I resorted to conversing with the *only one* who is capable of knowing all the answers. I prayed that God would still my anger, quiet my anxieties and direct my necessary moves.

Back in Chapter 3, I referenced a Captain who used every possible means to have me terminated at my first year anniversary. At this point in my career, Captain Ferrell has retired and moved out of town. Captain Ferrell is a bright man and before his retirement was Assistant Chief.

After my seniority dilemma reached the stage of filing a complaint with the Civil Service Commission, Captain Ferrell called my home saying, "I hear that you are in need of help in regard to procedure and facts surrounding this seniority issue."

I responded, "I certainly would appreciate any help I could get due to the fact that I had no facts regarding the initial restructuring."

Captain Ferrell said, "I think I can help. Let me do some leg work and some snooping to gain necessary facts to aid in writing your civil service complaint."

I graciously accepted his offer. I hung up the phone in total shock. Immediately I praised and thanked our Heavenly Father for His intervention.

With the information gained through the captain's efforts, the Civil Service Commission restored my lost years.

God has a plan—look how many people participated.

THIRTEEN

The Forces of Evil Aren't Always Dark

*Job 28:28—"And to man He said, 'Behold, the fear of the Lord, that is
wisdom; And to depart from evil is understanding.' " (NIV)*

At the time when my first husband left me, my boys were
ages 3 and 18 months. I lived in a boarding house set up for
single mothers. When I entered the doors to this large home, it
was arranged so that each mother could share a room with her
children and yet utilize the living room and kitchen as common
areas of the house.

With our admittance, there were five mothers and eleven
children living there, which included Rose and her son, Bo. Rose
a drill-sergeant type woman, whom I grew to love very dearly,
operated this house.

When I say that Rose was the Marine type Sergeant I am not
tugging anyone's toes. She had very regimental rules. For
instance, she washed all the clothes, and folded them and we
were left only with the task of taking them to our rooms and
putting them away. She cared for our children in the daytime and

prepared all the meals while we worked. Rose made wonderful, healthy meals that came with rules.

Rule # 1 – There will be no talking at the dinner table, which in reality was a very large picnic table.

Rule #2 – There was no beverage served with the meal. Rose had found that children drank their milk, and/or juice and then could not eat their meal. We could drink our beverages after we cleaned up our plates.

Rule #3 – No one left the table without being excused. The rules applied to the mothers and children equally.

We lived at Rose's for a little over a year. In that time, I became very endeared to Rose. After all, I did not have anywhere else to live and she was a great deal of help to the boys and I. I literally believed that she saved my life and made it possible for me to keep my children. I did not have the option of going home to my parents.

When I became a part of the City Police Department, Rose was very proud and felt that she had contributed to my desire to better myself and to do whatever it took to support and care for my boys.

While living in the house with Rose, she often spoke about spiritual phenomena that I didn't understand nor did I want to. She mentioned once that she had the capability of calling down fireballs from heaven and that she could take care of (in other words deal with) people by just speaking it into existence. Several years later when I was transferred to the night shift, this was going to cause a great deal of inconvenience for my household and especially for our young daughter. Rose called me on the phone and asked me if I would drop by and visit with her. When I did so, she went into an absolute tirade about the injustice that the Command was doing to us. She wanted me to grant her permission to "take care" of those responsible and work toward getting this travesty reversed.

With great fervor I responded, "No Rose you must not use any form of spiritual power that does not come from the hand of God against my superiors." I explained in detail that I had given my life over to the control of Jesus and that if I were to be relieved of uniform duty that He would see to it. She agreed, but very reluctantly.

As long as I knew Rose she had an emergency monitoring device in her home. She ran it day and night. She listened and paid close attention to the calls of all of the emergency agencies. Therefore, when I was transferred to nights and when she could not sleep, she paid close attention to where I was and what I was doing. Often she would call me and ask questions about the welfare of an officer that had been in an altercation. She was always concerned about people's well-being. On many occasions as I would start a shift, Rose would call me and ask if I would take my first coffee break and stop and visit her. Whenever possible I would walk in her back door and join her in the living room for coffee in the middle of the night.

Whenever it was possible to attend church on Sunday, I would invite Rose to join us and many times she would. She started questioning her "powers" and even told me that she thought they were wrong as they could be used for bad rather than for good.

One evening in 1995 after I left St. Luke's hospital and headed toward home. I heard a still, small voice tell me to stop and pray with Rose. Even though Rose had attended church with us a few times, I did not find her receptive at all to surrendering her life to the Lord nor asking him to rule and guide her life. So, when I felt this prompting, I was very reluctant to obey even though I was just a few blocks from her home. Therefore, I convinced myself that I was only hearing my own thought processes and I continued my trek home.

Three or four more blocks passed when I heard the same still, small, not even demanding voice say, "Go back and pray with Rose."

I came to the next intersection, turned right, turned right again at the alley and headed to Rose's house. I entered the back door, walked through the kitchen and found Rose in the living room. She took one look at me and said, "I wondered when you were going to stop. I'm ready to pray with you."

I did and she did and just two or three months later Rose took a fast trip home to be with Jesus.

God has a plan and I am so thankful that His still small voice allowed me to be a part of it.

FOURTEEN
Shock Treatment

Deuteronomy 31:6—"Be strong and courageous, do not be afraid or tremble at them, for the LORD your God is the one who goes with you. He will not fail you or forsake you." (NIV)

Welcome to the World of Nights! I hope to describe for you an accurate picture of the world after the lights go out. I only trust I can give due justice to reality.

My very first night on the shift and I was early. My gear; briefcase, ticket books, PR24 baton, flashlight, etc. were already positioned by a chair in the last row of the roll call room. I think that if I sit as far back as possible no one will notice that I am even there. Feeling totally out of place, like confetti at a funeral, I vacated the roll call room. I made my way to the Record's room knowing that I will see a friendly face there. As I am waiting for the evening clerk to return I hear voices from around the corner where the Command Office is situated. I recognized the voice of my Lieutenant telling my Sergeant and my Captain, "It is bad enough we have to have all those women on this Department but even worse, I get this slut on my shift." It didn't take too much analyzing to realize that he was speaking of *me*.

I am sure that those reading this are thinking. She should immediately without missing a beat report this to their command. In my defense, I remind you that I have tried in the past. I have reported or made attempts to report infractions and have been shot down in one form or another.

So in an attempt to equalize the emotion that I was experiencing, I went straight to the women's restroom where I could be far away from his hurling accusations. I spoke with my Lord who I knew loved me. I said, "Father I know that I have been made in your image and don't have to accept that description of myself. I also know that I can do all things through your Son, Jesus. Lord you already know what enormous fear I have and I ask that you give me confidence to return to roll call and help me to forget the degradation that was just put upon me." I regained my composure and returned to roll call, gaining determination but also adding to already overflowing bitterness.

First night–Roll Call–ever watch *Hill Street Blues*? Our roll call was reminiscent of theirs except that in the early '80s profane language was not commonplace on TV. So our roll call sounded a little more crass.

The previous day I had worked in a safe and serene Crime Prevention Division where everyone knew that I loved Jesus. Out of respect, they–most of the time–refrained from obscenities, sexual innuendos, lewd gestures and unwanted propositions.

Twenty- four odd hours later, I am in a roll call room listening to profanity the likes of which I had not heard since my childhood while working in the barnyard. "Is this for real? This isn't really happening! What a gross room of people!! Buck up Jane, you're going to be here for a long, long time."

By now my constitution had made the decision that I was going to survive the night shift if I had to do it standing on my head at 4th and Main Street.

I attended recruit training twelve years prior to this. While the guys were learning routine patrol procedures, traffic training, and combat procedures, I was sent to the Juvenile Division with the explanation, "You will never work Uniform thus you aren't required to attend these sessions. Prior to April 1, 1984 I had never sat behind the wheel of a marked squad car.

This fateful April Fools Day I was assigned to work with Officer Sean as my Field Training Officer. My Field Training Officer was about six feet tall. My first impression was that he was a strong, gruff, stalwart man of few words. He made it quite obvious that he wasn't given a choice in regard to "training me," so, sit down, be quiet and just listen.

With equal conviction, I informed him that I had been given no choice of trainer either. I had never met Officer Sean, even though we had been a part of the same department with only six months separating us. I might add, however, that Officer Sean ALWAYS looked like he had swallowed a dill pickle sideways. My most prevalent thought was "How in Our Mighty Lord's green earth was I going to survive this?"

At the end of day one, I glimpsed a mere twinkle at the end of a very long black tunnel. My initial assessment of my Training Officer was now sprinkled with kindness, consideration, and I thought that I might have momentarily spotted a little compassion. I was certain I could return tomorrow.

The "normal" department Field Training Program consisted of approximately two to four months with a Field Training Officer and then a period of time on your own with the Training Officer covering your calls. I was given a whopping five days with Officer Sean. Upon completion of that week, Officer Sean was responsible to turn in an evaluation report regarding my performance, to the Watch Lieutenant.

This evaluation was not discussed with me nor did I know that it existed. After the fact, I was told that the Lieutenant reviewed the report. He then returned it to Officer Sean and told him to rewrite the report. His claim was that Sean had evaluated me way too favorably. (Now, I've been thinking that some of the Command may actually want me discouraged to the point of "I Quit". I keep thinking, "4th & Main St.").

Night after night I would go home from the shift feeling rejected by the supervisory personnel. All of my prior employments had been peppered with praise and total acceptance. I was now feeling like a dirty mop just after having the water squeezed out. Could this nightmare possibly get any worse?

My Training Officer was relieved of his Training Officer status because he chose to remain true to his sincere evaluation. His explanation was that the evaluation form did not apply accurately to me as I was new to uniform work but my other police skills were already firmly established.

I was handed off to another Training Officer for one night and a different Officer for two nights. Both of these seasoned Officers said I was nowhere near ready to work a District on my own.

Voilà! My ninth night on the street I was out in a car by myself in District 2–the prostitute, skid row area of town.

After roll call and assignment of Districts, the Uniform Officers proceed with their gear to the ramp parking lot and positioned said gear into their assigned car. Here comes another bitterness builder. I am assigned one of the oldest cars. It operates on propane gas. No one wants to drive these cars, and they are assigned by seniority. I have very little seniority remember. In reality I was third in seniority.

I packed my gear in the car and quickly check; overheads, flashers, siren, radio, flashlight, front and back seats for possible contraband left by those arrested by previous shift officer who used this car. Ten minutes later, my car is ready to leave the station. Wait a minute!

Last night at the end of my shift, anticipating being on my own the following day, I have one of my panic chats with God. It went something like this. I told Him about the–too numerous to count–fears I had regarding handling a District alone.

I complained to Him about my lack of training. I grumbled about the Command's attitude. I told Him I was afraid of the dark. I mentioned inadequacies, insecurities, lack of combat strategies and unknown enemies. I talked with Him about all my unknowns in regard to traffic codes, procedures, etc. When I exhausted myself in negative confessions, into my remembrance popped His words: "I shall never leave you nor forsake you. Surely goodness and mercy will follow you all the days of your life. You can do all things through Christ who strengthens you. I will be with you always." Then He spoke to my heart and said, "I will go with you—invite me."

My memory restored, I invited my Lord Jesus to share the front seat of my squad car. Never again did fear overtake me. Did I ever fear? Yes, but I believe just enough to keep me cautious and aware.

For the thirteen remaining years of my career, I did not forget to ask my Lord to accompany me in the front seat and to guide and guard me. His plan is perfect and I want to be a part of it.

FIFTEEN
The World After Dark

Romans 13:12—The night is nearly over; the day is almost here. So let us put aside the deeds of darkness and put on the armor of light. (NIV)

We really do view the world through rose-colored glasses especially if we have not been nocturnal by nature. Prior to my Watch III experience, I was known to comment, "A crook is a crook", intimating that one is just the same as the other. I then commenced to find that the night-variety of criminals are more belligerent, more rude, more devious, and much more dangerous.

The same people I dealt with while working days seemed like kittens compared to their night persona. The transformation from kittens to mountain lions is not an exaggeration. Consequently, the mannerisms used to deal with the day criminal had to be altered accordingly. My kind, soft spoken, but firm authority, graduated to harsh, loud and demanding.

Travel back with me to my first night alone in District 2, the area of prostitutes and skuzzy bars. From 10:30 to midnight the calls were not too intimidating. Shortly after midnight, the dispatcher breaks the silence and says, "D-2 & D-4?" My response, "D-2, W7th and Sperry, go ahead." D-4 responds from East 4ᵗʰ and Sanoah. (miles away). The communications operator then replies, "Go to Sook and W 7ᵗʰ Streets in regard to a female who has been stabbed. I'm trying to get a description of the suspect now." D-4 and I acknowledge. I'm using my calm voice but I'm thinking, "now what do I do?" I wonder if they would notice if I just took the rest of the night off?

Maybe I should just not answer the radio any more. While all these wonderings are going on in my head, I am driving to the call location, which was only 6 or 7 blocks away. I have now pulled up in front of a fleabag bar. "What do I do now? Do I get out of my car and go inside without my cover car? Or should I wait until he gets here? If I wait, I'll be criticized for being a chicken". Oh well, I'll go in – There is a woman in there who may be bleeding to death." I put on my -know what I'm doing face– and confidently walk into this dark, dingy, smelly bar.

Once inside, I see a 40-ish white female on the floor near the bar. Her throat has been cut from ear to ear. Directly behind me is the ambulance crew. I head to the bar to gain information from the bartender.

I am given the information regarding the suspect's physical description and possible vehicle that he left in. I relay this information to communications who in turn dispatches it to the other cars.

As I attempt to put my radio back into the leather holder at my waist, I am very roughly grabbed from behind. I now find myself up against a wall with hands at my throat. The attacker was none other than the D-4 Officer. His authoritative comments were, "What in the hell is the matter with you? Don't ever do this again." I am feeling very defensive as he continues his tirade. "What good would you be to me if I came in here and you were lying next to the victim, in the same condition?" She was dead by the way.

I apologized and thanked him for frightening me into a learning experience that I would not soon forget.

This set of facts, combined with coffee and dinner chats revealed my total lack of procedure knowledge and led my loyal peers into taking turns teaching me the necessary tools to continue to exist on the night shift. Nightly, during the hours when calls were sparse, they would take me to a deserted part of the city and show me how to stop traffic, how to handle felony stops and many other techniques. They rehearsed with me what to do when there was a weapon or the possibility of one involved in a call.

One scenario after another was created to help me feel adequate and just a little more confidant. My peers grumbled, as I was barely trained and expected to handle a District by myself.

Three weeks now I'd worked D-2 on my own. At 11:30 P.M. one night, my Lieutenant spoke to me by radio and said, "D-2?" I replied with the normal, "Go ahead." He requested, "Meet me at 3rd and Gable Street." And I responded with the affirmative reply, "10-4".

At 3rd and Gable, I positioned my squad car next to his in order that we were speaking directly at each other. He informed me that he had a document that needed my signature. I expected to see a report that I failed to sign. After he handed the paperwork to me, I turned on my reading light and immediately noticed that this is not a report that I wrote needing a signature.

I read, "I agree that I am technically well enough trained to adequately work the street." Below this statement was a signature line. I could not even come close to describing the arousal of anger that came over me for this "cover your hind end" gesture.

I simply handed it back and said that I refused to put my signature on a paper containing a statement that I had numerous times denied. I had many times voiced my displeasure in regard to my lack of training. Just before he pulled away in a huff, he shouted, "Well you will sign this paper. I'll see to it."

My reply was simply, "Hey, suspend me for whatever time you deem appropriate but I am not signing that paper."

Neither the paper nor the conversation was ever mentioned again. I added more bitterness to my stack and topped it off with a nice chunk of resentment. As I'm seething with what I think is a righteous form of hatred, (isn't that a laugh) I hear the Lord speak to my heart, "You need to forgive him." Of course I didn't comply.

God has a plan and obviously I'm squelching my part of it.

SIXTEEN

Stories

Lamentations 3:22-23—Because of the LORD's great love we are not consumed, for his compassions never fail. They are new every morning; great is your faithfulness. (NIV)

September of every year marked the beginning of the Annual Basic Skills School. This was a required event for all officers regardless of rank. While the leaves were turning gorgeous shades of yellow, coral and red, we were seeing nothing but crisp dried up corn stalks. The training facility and driving and shooting ranges were out in the middle of farmland. Once inside the facility we felt as though we were planted beside someone's crops, patiently waiting for harvest.

Prior to working in Uniform, while participating in department-oriented schools, I diligently listened to what the "guys" would call war stories. Some of these "stories" were humorous, some of them pathetic, some of them frightening, and a great number of them enormously sad. However, they were their stories. Although there were "plainclothes" stories too, in my mind, those stories did not compare in content to the uniform accounts (first line stories).

So, after a few weeks and months, I begin to realize that I was building a diary of my own "stories." When I say "my stories," I strictly mean that this is the way that I perceived the incident.

During my tenure, I learned swiftly that if there were five officers at a call we could expect to hear five separate versions of the occurrence over our next break. Please keep this in mind as you read on. All calls are serious and have their solemn side. However, the actions and reactions sometime make for great copy.

This set of circumstances requires a prelude. The troops would often say that I was far too even-tempered. At times they felt that the conclusion too many of my calls should have ended in one or more arrests. In other words, I gave too many breaks.

My explanation, although far lengthier than what is written here, simply said that unless a serious infraction occurred, people could sometime benefit more from a situation if an arrest were not made. The time is 1:30 AM on a calm (weather-type calm), but busy night. It seems that the complainant came home drunk to find that his apartment had been burglarized. The location of the incident was in a low rent district of town and there was not a cover car available. I arrived at the location and followed the directions given by the dispatcher to find the apartment. "Go to the North/South alley, located on the West side of the address given. Using the North door, enter and proceed to the basement area of the dwelling unit."

I followed the instructions competently. This was not my first attempt at finding "out-of the-way apartments." This time, however, there actually was no apartment, just an open basement in this apartment house.

The complaining party's household items were scattered all over this basement, which obviously was accessible to anyone who lived in the building. The complainant, George, started barking at me as I started down the stairs. "Can't you cops keep an eye on anything? Ish unbelievable that all you haves to do ish pick up peoples for drunk driving."

I am now aware that I am speaking with one of those drunks. He then starts to holler at me. "YOU DIRTY ROTTEN F****** COP. IT TOOK YOU FOREVER TO GET HERE AN IN THE MEANTIME THE THIEVES MADE OFF WITH MY STUFF."

I said, "George let's lower your voice and just give me the information necessary to make a report." I then picked up his name through the slurred speech.

He started in again. "YOU COPS ARE ALL P***KS. (I can't print that word) YOU DON'T REALLY CARE ABOUT US – YOU F***ERS (I can't print that word either) JUST WANT TO PUT PEOPLE IN JAIL."

Kindly I responded, "George, I refuse to sit here and listen to you run down my profession and those of us in it–So I am going to ask you again to give me a list of the items that are missing from your belongings."

Upon which he gave me a list of two items, a TV and a microwave. He then started in with the hollering and the name-calling. While using his loudest voice, he started to stand up and when he did so, the chair he was sitting on came flying at me.

I had been writing and not looking at him. I naturally assumed that he was throwing the chair at me. I quickly grabbed my lapel microphone and requested a second car at my location. By now I was standing and confronting him about this chair. (I'm not sure why I am confronting him.

He is about six foot, four inches and a muscular biker type and I am five foot, seven inches, not muscular and my type is chicken). As I start to replay this scenario it is obvious to me that when this man stood up, the chain attached to his wallet caught on the chair and thus the reason I thought he was throwing it at me. I then cancel my request for a second car.

I finish up my report and leave the building. As I am doing so, George follows me all the way up the stairs still calling me a pig and many other names that I am unable to put into print. When I exit the apartment house into the alley, there sits a fellow officer in his car as he had just arrived. When he sees this scene, he asks me why I have not arrested this man. I tell him that he and his cohorts are far too quick to arrest and beyond that, it is time to go to breakfast and I don't want to spend an hour at the jail.

As I walk toward my squad car, which is approximately ten feet away, George and Officer Maron are to my back. George is walking toward a pick up truck and apparently intends to drive away. I then hear Officer Maron on the air asking if there is an ASAP (Alcohol Safety Action Program) car in the vicinity and if so please come to our location. I walked back to Maron's car and tell him that we cannot let George get into that pickup and attempt to drive away. I approach George and tell him to go back into the apartment and call it a night. I cancel the ASAP car, which shows up anyway.

I proceed to fill in the blanks for the ASAP officer. George starts to walk toward the apartment but first stops at Officer Maron's vehicle and has some parting words. Officer Maron is out of his car and scuffling with George.

I returned to his car and jokingly say to him. "Maron, you couldn't possibly have let him go into his apartment and just sleep it off. No you had to make sure that he ended up arrested and I have to take him to jail."

Officer Maron did not have him cuffed yet when he said, "Well he called you a F*****G C***T (very bad words)."

A speaker went off in my head saying, "Can the compassion, cancel the breaks, forget supper, this sucker needs to go to jail." I turned instantly furious. I lost all of my normal calm and amicability. I grabbed this beast, George, and with Maron's help landed him on the hood of the car. Handcuffs were out and on his wrists in no time. I then marched him to the rear seat of my squad car. All of this time the ASAP officer was watching this in great amusement. Before I could explain the circumstances, the ASAP officer, known for his wit, got out of his car, sauntered to the back door of my squad, put his head into the back seat and said, "Congratulations fella, someone finally pissed her off." He then strode back to his car. I got behind the wheel and informed the dispatcher that I was en route to the jail with a male prisoner.

I get about a block away from the jail and George mumbles, "Hey lady, besides that, you are super ugly." I replied, "Just the same, fella, this is no beauty contest and you are going to jail."

The following shift I was called out of roll call and dispatched to a "man down" call. You know the "I've fallen and I can't get up" routine.

When I arrived I found a male, approximately 20 years of age. He was so wasted that I literally had to peel him off the ground and into my squad car. There were several groans and grunting noises but no conversation. I proceeded to transport him to jail. After a short period of time I could hear him murmuring in the back seat. I said, "Sir you are going to have to speak up as I cannot hear you."

He loudly proclaimed, "Madam, you are jush absholutely bootiful."

I thanked him and drove on.

He said, "I's meant it. You are jush shtunnin." With or without the compliments, he went to jail. Visualize the confused state of my mind when just the night before I was told how super ugly I was. It's a good thing not to take too seriously what is said from the back seat of a squad car.

In our state, the bars closed at 2:00 A.M. I was dispatched to a disturbance at an all-night restaurant. The communications person said that a male was sitting at the counter, stacking glasses and giving the waitresses a tough time. My cover car was quite a way off. I entered the restaurant, which was just packed with people. I approached a man sitting at the counter who was stacking glasses. I asked him if he would accompany me outside to visit about this. He immediately looked at me and proclaimed, "I hate waitresses." I explained to him that he couldn't be collecting the used glasses from the restaurant to build pyramids. I initially assumed that he was drunk. I asked him if he had been drinking and he adamantly stated that he was not drunk and had not been drinking. I then told him that I needed to collect some information in order to fill out a police report. I asked his name. He said, "I hate waitresses and so I am not going to answer your questions."

I informed him that I was not a waitress and so he could answer my questions. He then said that I was actually a waitress disguised as a police officer. My cover officer entered the scene at this point and, not realizing the complexion of the situation, agreed with this nut. He said, "You got that right fella, she's a waitress."

At this time, this guy just went berserk. A Sergeant showed up on the scene and it took all three of us to contain him. The Sergeant suggested that the man be taken to the hospital to keep from hurting himself, as he had not really broken any laws. While transporting him to the hospital, this man asked me several times for a cigarette.

I politely told him that I don't smoke. He then told me that all good restaurants sell cigarettes and thus I should be able to go to a machine and buy him some.

He then started to talk like Morse Code: "Dee deet, da da deet, dot, dot deet, do, do deet,"

Officer Ossie (the cover car) followed me to the hospital. When we exited the squad car, the prisoner asked Officer Ossie for a cigarette. Officer Ossie gave him one as we waited to go into the hospital. The man smoked approximately 3/4s of the cigarette. He then sucked it into his mouth and swallowed it. He then started the "Dee deet, da da deet, dot, dot, deet, do, do, deet," again. All the time he was reciting the Morse code, he was getting closer and closer to Officer Ossie until he was nose to nose with Officer Ossie. The notes to be added to this report became easier to write in regard to this man's destination.

At the beginning of another extremely busy night, I received a call of a domestic disturbance. There was no cover car available. I went to the address and found a husband and wife in a vicious argument. I received my first explanation from the husband who was very visibly drunk. I then went to the kitchen where I found the wife with two daughters.

All over the walls, floor, counters and stove was noodle soup. On the burner was a very large pot, which still contained noodle soup. The wife informed me that when her husband became enraged, he took the pot and just started splattering soup toward the walls, the appliances and the occupants.

While in the kitchen I radioed the dispatcher to check for any "wanteds" on this husband. Before I left the kitchen I was informed that they had warrants for this man and that I had a rookie coming to cover me. The wife had already informed me that her husband had a gun in their bedroom.

I walked into the living room and told the man, "We have warrants for your arrest. I will have to take you down to the station. Please turn around and put your hands behind your back."

Instantly he complied. I put one wrist in the cuff when the front door opened and my rookie cover came in. At this the husband decided that he did not want to be handcuffed. He wanted to go get socks and shoes in the bedroom. I said no and then the fight was on. He started swinging the handcuff at me and trying to push me away. I kept a hold of him and was working very hard to keep him from landing in the middle of the living room that was adorned with a large round glass coffee table. While I was tussling with this man, my cover was standing there watching me.

I finally steered my prisoner around the table and he landed on the couch, face down, with me on top of him attempting to get his hands out from in front of him in order to finish handcuffing him. He refused and was way too big for me to move so I removed my stun gun and planted it on his thigh. He instantly put his hands behind his back and I completed the handcuffing.

I then forcefully asked my rookie cover to get over here and help me get him upright, which he did. In the process of getting him to his feet, his pants fell down. I told the other Officer to take him just as he was to his squad car and to transport him to jail. He refused and physically pulled the man's pants up before transporting him.

You may imagine the sight. I didn't want to see him with or without pants. The following morning this man who was six foot four, 240 lbs, filed a police brutality complaint against me.

During the years that I worked the night shift, my boys were in the age group of 22 to 24. Their friends spent a great deal of time at our house while growing up. They ate a lot of meals in our home. The Lord was always shared with them even when they weren't always so receptive.

I disapproved of my boys or their friends frequenting alcohol-serving establishments. So I would leave little notes on their vehicles when I spotted them parked in locations anywhere near these institutions. They would often tell me that it was very embarrassing to find a note under the windshield after leaving the local bar. Especially when the communication was signed Mother. The moment was even more awkward if they had a date.

These notes often read like this, "Call your Mother. She is in fierce pain due to the amount of time that she needs to spend praying to keep you out of these types of establishments. Love, Mother."

I often left similar notes on their friends' cars. One young man who was the continued recipient of these notes would seldom comment but just smile at me after receiving "the ever present note."

He was gone for quite some time with the Air National Guard. He had been deployed during Desert Storm. I missed leaving him notes. At the end of a shift one evening I came to the parking lot to get into my personal car and found a note under the windshield wiper. It simply said, "I'm back." And it was signed J.

One night a young man came home with our son, Larry, to spend the night. We ate supper together and we had a tradition of having a very short devotion after supper. While I was preparing the meal Larry came to me and asked, "May we skip the devotion tonight, Mom? Matt doesn't go to church and he would be so embarrassed if we did that."

I kindly responded, "We won't change our schedule but I will make it short and will not request much discussion."

Although he wasn't pleased that it wasn't going to be scratched altogether, he was at least relieved that it was not going to be a lengthy session. After dinner I read the devotion and it was apparent that the devotion elicited a response. Matt took off, giving us his thoughts and asking all kinds of questions. After his questions were answered, the boys were dismissed and left the table. Shortly thereafter Larry came running up the stairs and related that Matt just loved the devotion time and was really glad that we had not skipped it.

One evening we were called to a fight in progress at a local nightclub. I entered with three other Officers. As we walked through the bar and tables toward the back where the fight was still raging, I kept hearing–"Hi Mom, Hello Ma, Lookin good Ma, I didn't do it Mom, Hey Mom."

One of my peers turned around and said to me, "Just exactly how many kids do you have?"

During their teen years, the boy's friends spent a great deal of time at our house and they all called me Mom. For some reason, they all thought that it might help them someday to have a Mom that was also a Cop.

In the same set of circumstances, after having been dispatched to a different nightclub a year or so later, I was entering the Club ahead of about four other Officers. As we approached, several young people were flocking out the door, obviously knowing that the police were on their way. As one young man exited, he grabbed me by the front of my shirt and pushed me up against the wall. I was facing the Officers behind this young man. Fortunately for him I had a large smile on my face as they all had PR-24 batons aimed at his knees.

Of course the young man was a son, who liked to tease me often about the fact that he could "take me." This time, his attempt to overpower me almost lost him a kneecap or two.

One night I was working the dreaded desk, this was directly inside the station and the occupant of "the desk" had to take all the calls made to the regular police number and a great deal of them were complaints. A deputy Sheriff brought a young man into the station, handcuffed and headed for the Alcohol Safety Action Room where they test for level of alcohol.

I was not paying any attention as they walked by and all of the sudden I heard a male voice say, "Hi Ma."

I was immediately disturbed and my heart sank thinking that one of my boys had been picked up while drinking. I looked up quickly to see one of the boy's friends looking back at me. The officer following him was well known for giving "no one" a break.

I left the station about 3:30 AM to go to breakfast. This deputy had breakfast with a group of us each morning and when I arrived he informed me with no fanfare, "I charged your friend with public intoxication and saw that he got home."

The following day my son called me and said, "I hear that Samson was arrested last night."

I replied, "Yes and he got off very easily compared to what could have happened to him."

My son said, "Yeh, Samson said he finally talked the Deputy out of charging him more severely."

My response was, "He can thank the Lord for protecting him this time. Next time he might not be so fortunate."

Yes I know God has a plan. He uses so many to fulfill them.

SEVENTEEN

Dark November Night

Luke 11: 33-35—"No one lights a lamp and puts it in a place where it will be hidden, or under a bowl. Instead he puts it on its stand, so that those who come in may see the light. Your eye is the lamp of your body. When your eyes are good, your whole body also is full of light. But when they are bad, your body also is full of darkness. See to it, then, that the light within you is not darkness. (NIV)

It was November, the night air was fresh and long sleeves were required in order to remain comfortably warm. After the sun set, the temperature dropped significantly and, in order to keep the chill off, a heavy sweater was necessary.

At 2300 hours, I was working D-9, an area of about 10 square miles. The radio dispatcher called for D-9 and D-10. I respond, "Go ahead for D-9." Carol, the communications operator, waits for D-10 to answer before dispatching the call. After his response, she sends us to 27th and Jay streets where a 20 year old, male, is in a house with a gun. We are told that he is depressed and has been terrifying the occupants and at the same time threatening to commit suicide.

D-10 and I arrive in the area at approximately the same time. Policy dictated that we not pull our cars into the immediate block due to the nature of the call. D-10 parked his vehicle approximately one block south of the 10-23 or the location of the call. I parked about 1 block west of the reported residence.

While driving, I had a tendency to get very warm as I had the heater going most of the time. Most night shift officers operated similarly, eliminating the bulk of the regulation, heavy, leather jacket. We cruised in shirtsleeves and put our coats on, if necessary, when we went out on calls.

On this occasion, both Officer Ossie and I locked our squad cars, remained coatless and left both cars running. About ½ block south of the location Officer Ossie and myself met at the intersection. We purposely stayed on the west side of the street, where there were little or no streetlights. We tried to stay close to the houses, rather than near the sidewalk in order that we were not seen. Carol had informed us, that the subject with the gun had left the house and was now in the middle of Jay Street.

We were nearly one half-block away from the young man when he spotted us. I couldn't see that I had gloves on but his vision of us was perfect as we clamored our way through the neighborhood shrubbery. When he acknowledged us, he insisted that we leave him alone while he alternated waving his gun at us and then pointed it at himself.

This young man immediately started backing into a playground area, which put a very high fence between him and us. My immediate thought was that this fence was in no way going to work as a shield for us if bullets started flying. The only other solid, tangible item between he and us was a pickup truck. Good thing, right? Not so good, it was a Chevy S-10 pickup. The only area that could block bullets was the motor block and I alone am bigger than that. Officer Ossie is six foot seven or eight and on his knees, he would not be protected.

We went right into our negotiating techniques. We both looked at each other and said, "You can start."

Unfortunately, it was my district so I was forced to take the lead. I started asking this young man what could have compelled him into this position. He related a relationship problem, lack of direction, lack of work and lack of family understanding. At this point, I wanted to either cry or go out onto that playground and slap that boy as I was getting frightfully cold.

However, I did use all the restraint that I could muster and talked with him like a Mother and told him that he was really loved and that families are not always understanding or perfect. In spite of all of his misgivings, life is really worth living.

Intermittently, this young man would point his 357 magnum at us and threaten to shoot us. He did not know that we had training and that we knew that all he really wanted was to force us into shooting him as he was unable to do so himself. Policy also states that you can't do that. (Shoot him I mean.)

Now it was Officer Ossie's turn to attempt to break down the barrier of despair that had this young fellow trapped out there in that playground. Officer Ossie talked and I prayed silently, "Lord, please speak to this young person to give up that gun and leave with us peacefully." Then just to be safe I silently prayed "Set that gun down in the name of Jesus."

Now it was my turn to do the talking and I don't talk well, just standing still, so I talk and start walking away from the cab of that pickup. About three feet from the cab, these giant arms came out and grabbed me and pulled me back into the (not so safe) harbor behind the cab of this eensy-teensy pickup. At this point, we were being informed through lapel mikes that there were officers stationed on the ground around the perimeter of the playground with guns ready in the event that the situation turned sour.

I'm shivering and finding it difficult to talk. Officer Ossie's lips are turning purple and he is about to take the next turn at talking sense into this disturbed young man, who had the gun in his mouth one minute and was pointing it at us the next. Officer Ossie went into the next stage of negotiations, offering professional help. It was again my job to pray. Silently didn't work so I begin whispering, "Father in heaven, I am so cold, and numb, please guide us to bring this situation to an end. Send your Holy Spirit to minister peace to this young man, who is so upset, that he would consider killing himself." And then added, "Put that gun down in the name of Jesus."

My turn to talk. By this time I was ready to walk out onto that field and snatch him bald. I'm cold, I've missed coffee, my car is running out of gas, and I'm probably going to get a suspension for letting it run anyway. But I switch into compassionate mode and start talking and walking. This time I got almost to the tailgate before the long arm dragged me back.

I heard a message on the lapel mike. The Lieutenant was in a house about a block away and was about to set up a command post. We had, as yet, not received any instruction. Not that we expected to, but I was curious as to what they were going to do in the command post.

Another urgent message, this time it was Carol. "D-9 & D-10?"

I said, "Go ahead for D-9 and D-10." The Chief had been notified and he said that if things got any worse, he would come down."

I looked at Officer Ossie and said, "Would it be worse if you or I were lying on the ground?"

Officer's response, to my question was, "Let's get this over with. Two hours is long enough."

I said, "Your turn to talk, my turn to pray."

I never heard a word that Officer Ossie said from that point on as I had determined that God was going to hear me and I decided, in this case, whispering did not reach the ear of the Lord. Therefore, while he was talking, I was praying, not just aloud, but loud. I don't remember the text of that prayer; I only remember that it was fervent and serious.

Officer Ossie would occasionally take his eyes off the young man in the playground and look at me as though he were going to call for two ambulances when this ended. I just kept praying. I ended with, "Give up that gun in the name of Jesus."

From the North, we heard a vehicle enter the block, not imagining for a minute that a squad didn't have that intersection blocked. Looking up we saw a uniform car pull right into the area, right over the curb and into the playground, about 30 feet from the young man with the gun. Sergeant Fred steps out of his car and said, "Young man, hand that gun over to me right now."

Officer Ossie and I stand there astonished as this frightened young man came around and handed his weapon to the Sergeant.

Another car arrived on the scene and took this young man to the hospital for care, if needed, before he was arrested. Sergeant Fred picked up the radio and said, "Suspect in custody, all cars may return to their districts."

I said to Officer Ossie, "Want to go to coffee?" He responded, "As soon as I go home and change my pants." Many years went by before Officer Ossie ever mentioned the impact that those prayers had on his life.

God has a plan and He times it perfectly.

EIGHTEEN
Where Do You Go When You Need A Friend?

John 15: 15—I no longer call you servants, because a servant does not know his master's business. Instead, I have called you friends, for everything that I learned from my Father I have made known to you. (NIV)

The busy nights go by fast. As a matter of fact when there was not much space between calls, daylight pokes its head out of the eastern sky before you realize that the city hall clock has passed midnight.

The slow nights though are filled with agony. This applies to all who work those ungodly hours that were meant for neither man nor beast. Nights are meant for sleeping and for most, even if you had a straight eight hours of sleep, when the darkness creeps onto the scene, our eyes long to close and our bodies anguish for relaxation.

For the Watch III Police Officer, relief from the yearning to relax, sleep, let down ones defenses isn't going to happen. Most day-sleeping officers may have four undisturbed hours of sleep, then go to court for a couple of hours and then have another three or four hours of sleep. For the ambitious officers who choose to write many tickets and strive to fulfill an arrest record, their sleep may be disturbed by two chances at court per day. Traffic Court takes place at approx. 9 AM (you have to be there by then but may not be called to testify or learn of a dismissal until 11:30) and then there are misdemeanor cases and felony cases that begin at approximately 2 PM.

Unfortunately, the attorneys are unable to take into consideration an officer's day off or any other factor when these cases are scheduled thus a night officer may eek out three hours of sleep all together. Of course, in order to garner those coveted hours, their families are left without their help, their presence or their companionship a great deal of the time.

When one has been deprived of the sustenance of sleep, one becomes irritable, quick tempered and many times unresponsive. One of the best antidotes for these characteristics is humor. Massive doses of humor saved many suffering from exhaustion, despair, deprivation and numerous periods of loneliness.

The face of such humor was presented in many forms. Roll calls were often the nights beginning point for humor. One particular evening as I was about to enter the roll call room a female officer passed me as she was exiting. Upon her clearing the doorway, it slammed so hard that the casing was broken loose from the doorframe.

I entered the room and said to the occupants, "Man you guys, what did you say to her?"

One of the guys told me, "We (there were three or four of them there) were simply conducting a survey. She didn't make it past the first question."

Knowing that it was one of the dumbest moves I could make, I said, "And the first question was?"

The surveyor said, "When you are experiencing PMS, do you write more or less tickets?" I just stood there momentarily and he said, "Well, aren't you going to answer that?"

I responded, "I didn't think you were asking me but since you are I will have to say that I can't speak for PMS but if you might like to change that to menopause I could probably address the question."

We experienced lots of laughs and no one bothered to request a serious answer to that question. Of course, I never thought they wanted a serious answer anyway.

The night shift was full of storms. These storms came in many forms: family disturbances, gang fights, bar brawls, rapes, child abuse, neglect of all sorts, burglary, robbery, and many forms of traffic problems. The most disturbing storms were, in my opinion, the in- fighting that lifted its ugly head in the form of inside police politics. I used to call it the inevitable carousel ride.

One night a policy said this and the next night it was completely different, depending upon who was in charge. If command was fighting with the Communications personnel, we were all expected to pick up that fight and be unkind, rude, and set ourselves completely apart from them.

This was not only relayed by inference, many times it was blatantly spoken. "You are not to talk with the Communications personnel except professionally by radio."

Now I firmly believed that these were the individuals who made certain that I had cover when I went on calls. They were the people who I depended upon for accurate information and I certainly did not intend to be rude and unkind to them. I had also made it a habit to pick up the newspaper, as soon as it was printed and deliver it to the Communications room.

One particular night I was met by the Lieutenant as I was delivering the newspaper and he said, "Give me that paper, you are not going to have anything more to do with these people except to answer the calls that they dispatch."

With bravery that I didn't feel, I refused to hand him the newspaper and I said, "Sir, you may have to suspend me then as I do not intend to take up your fight nor anyone else's. I have no gripes about the Communications employees so I intend to stay in contact with them."

There was no further comment nor was I summoned to the Chief's office so I decided that the issue was settled.

At that particular time there was a male officer on our shift who had a very difficult time putting together a sentence without using very profane language. Truthfully, I did not struggle with profanity near as much as I did when someone expressed himself by using the Lord's name in vain. I had two situations involving the profanity man.

One night, he came to accompany me as I was having coffee. Roll call had been over for a couple of hours. He sat down carrying a very stern, disgusted demeanor and said, "Jane, I was reprimanded tonight, severely, and ordered not to use any of the profane words again in roll call due to the fact that you are present."

I quickly informed him that I had not complained about his method of expression. He assured me that he was certain that I had not squealed but would I please use a particular four letter word the following night at roll call—several times. I told him that if I were prone to utilize that type of communication that I would be ever so happy to accommodate him. But, since I gave up that kind of vernacular, I would have to decline.

He was very polite and thanked me anyway. The next evening at roll call, he brought with him a stack of que cards with different profanities written on them and when he spoke, rather than use the words, he just lifted his flash cards. His point was made and I was spared reverting to my former self.

Years later, this same officer and I were working the day shift together and the Captain of the shift invited him to his office for a chat about his language. Only this time the Captain told him that I had forcefully complained about the profane comments that he made at roll call.

Again, he met me at coffee, and this time he believed that I had indeed grumbled to the Captain. I was very unnerved that a command person would accuse me in order to supervise his subordinates. I believed that the way to be a good Christian witness was by example. Therefore, although many times words and actions did make me cringe, I did not feel anywhere near perfect enough to judge them.

On this occasion, I was so disgusted with the Captain for lying about my involvement that I marched right into his office and informed him that although I was not soliciting any further profanity, I certainly would prefer it, to his daily usage of God's name in vain. Much to my surprise, he apologized and said that he would work on this shortcoming. He was not always known for owning up to his wrongs.

Without planning it I found a haven from all the storms, ever so briefly, by having coffee occasionally at St. Aloise's Hospital. It began when I first followed up on a traffic accident victim who was transported to the hospital.

Of course the victim was immediately being attended to and thus there were normally 30 to 40 minutes wait before I was able to complete the traffic report by obtaining information from the victim. If we were busy, we may have to leave and handle a call and return to the hospital to complete the prior report.

At any rate, while waiting I had the opportunity to meet so many concerned doctors, nurses, technicians, security, and even maintenance people. There were nights when the outdoor temperature was way below zero. I would arrive at the hospital, after standing in traffic at the scene of an accident, feeling so cold. I was always certain that I *must* have frostbite and perhaps would never feel my toes again. The scene would be set, to take off your shoes, wrap your feet in a blanket taken from the warmer, and have a cup of coffee while you wait. What a harbor from a storm.

One of those nights, I met Nurse Sara. She was one fast-moving human being. She stayed as thin as she was because she couldn't sit still when she was sitting still. At 4 AM during her break, she was not content to just have a cup of coffee. She had to be doing some type of needlework.

It took only a couple of conversations with Nurse Sara for me to recognize that she was different. All of the nurses were kind. All of the doctors were professional. But Nurse Sara, walked way beyond what one would expect from an emergency nurse. One night she and I started to converse about our faith–actually many nights we conversed about our faith.

This was a Saturday night and she said, "I sure wish I could go to church on Sunday morning but our church starts so late that I cannot stay awake that long."

I told her, "Hey come with me. We start at 8:30."

I was very surprised to see her there. Of course, we didn't hang around after church to converse as we both needed to get to bed.

That night at the hospital she said to me. "Hey you forgot to tell me that your church lasted that long. I could have gotten more sleep if I waited and went to my own church." However, next Sunday she was there again. We have become lifelong friends. Friendship is a welcomed harbor from the daily storms.

I was not the only officer that found St. Aloise's and their employees as a refuge. There were several other officers who gravitated there from time to time. Occasionally we would cross paths on calls and sometime we purposely went there for coffee. And I almost forgot there were the regular potlucks.

When this event took place, we were offered a special invitation to stop during our dinner breaks. What a treat–home cooked food–and so much of it. I did learn quickly that some liked "hot spicy" food. It did keep me warm and comforted from the storm.

One of the long nights as I was having coffee at St. Aloise's Hospital, I ran into an old friend from my sordid past. This young lady and I were very good friends twenty years prior to this and we had lost touch with each other. I knew her boys from a previous marriage. However, she had remarried and had children that I had never met. She informed me that her youngest son, age 13, was in the hospital with leukemia.

We made arrangements to have dinner the following afternoon. During our meal, we filled in the gaps with highlights of all those years. When we came to the subject of her son, Morey, she briefly told me of his battle and said that she would like me to meet him.

She also said, "I do have some guidelines about meeting him though." I asked her what those rules might be. She asserted, "I just want you to know that Morey is not very outgoing, nor affectionate. So, I appreciate it if you wouldn't do any of that hugging stuff. And, his Grandma is one of those religious types, therefore, he gets plenty of that kind of talk. So I would appreciate if you stay off the topic of religion and any references to faith."

I said, "Dee, you are really tying my hands here. I am not sure what I am going to be able to say to him at that rate."

She laughed at me and said, "I just want you to meet him and I would like you to pray for him. I just don't want to antagonize him."

We left the restaurant and headed to the hospital. En route, I prayed, "Lord, you will definitely have to intercede in this introduction and the ensuing conversation. Lord, I am not even sure why you would have me become acquainted with this young man. I just put my trust in you."

I admit that I was very nervous. Can you imagine, being anxious about meeting a 13-year-old?

Lying on the hospital bed was a young man behind a hospital mask. Dee introduced him to me and she went through the whole explanation of our long ago friendship and inserted that I was currently a Police Officer. Well, Morey was off and running with the questions. He wanted to know every detail about traffic arrests, drug questions, and juvenile laws vs. adult laws and on and on.

There were two other people in the room. We hardly noticed. I sat at the right side of his bed and we talked until I realized that I must hurry home to put on my uniform or I would be late for work. As I was explaining that I had to go, Morey said to me. Would you come over here a little closer? I stood up and idled closer to his bed. He lifted his finger and motioned for me to come closer. I bent down toward the bed. He quickly took off his mask and grabbed my neck and gave me a long, tight hug.

So much for the hands-off policy. As I was about to leave, Morey asked, "Jane there are a lot of nights when I am unable to sleep at all. Would it be possible for you to stop up and see me some of the nights that you work?"

I assured him that I would stop as often as I possibly could.

The following evening, prior to going to work, I stopped to see Morey. He had been on chemotherapy and when I arrived, he was trying to find someone who had a camera so that they could take a picture of him before his hair fell out. What a coincidence, I had my camera case in the back seat of my car. I went back to the parking lot and took lots of pictures of Morey with hair. He was so happy. For some reason, this was very important to him.

Many, many nights I stopped in Morey's room in the middle of the night. If we were not busy, I would talk with him until I was forced to leave. We just seemed to have a connection. Some type of bond pulled us together.

An evangelist was preaching at our church one evening and he mentioned that the following evening that he was going to be praying for healings. I knew that Monty would be unable to leave the hospital so I went and bought him a nice T-shirt. I took it with me to the front of the church when they prayed for healing. The evangelist prayed for Morey's healing and I remember so distinctly that he prayed that the Holy Spirit would touch Morey in a very special way.

Late that night or it might have been the early morning hours; I went to Morey's room to visit. He was wide-awake and was sitting up as though he were waiting for me to arrive. I scolded him for not trying to sleep and he said, "I couldn't wait for you to get here. I have to tell you what happened to me today. I was allowed to leave the hospital long enough to go to church so that I could be confirmed." He added, "You know that is when the Holy Spirit becomes a bigger part of your life."

I then presented him with his T-shirt and told him how the evangelist had asked God for the Holy Spirit to touch him. We both cried and knew that God had made His Presence known to Morey.

On the evening of the Policeman's Ball, Morey insisted that Brandon and I come to the hospital to see him. He said that he wanted to see us all duded up. I suspected that he wanted to say goodbye as we were leaving the following morning for a Pennsylvania vacation.

We modeled our good clothes and hugged Morey goodbye. I left the phone number at my brother's house in case he wanted to contact me and we were on our way to the ball. Starting to sound like Cinderella, aren't I?

We left early the next morning for Pennsylvania. Our plan was to spend three weeks on the East Coast. We toured a portion of the East with my brother and his wife and then we returned to their home. The day we returned to PA, Morey called in the evening. I tried to keep the anxiety from my voice, as I was concerned due to the long distance phone call. I asked him if he was all right. He said that he was. He just wanted to call and tell me that he loved me and that he appreciated our times together. He said when I returned home that he would be in Iowa City as he was going to have his bone marrow transplant.

The following day we left for home. As we approached Iowa City, I called Morey's family to see where he might be located at the hospital there. I was told that he had passed away the night before.

My heart was broken and at the very same time, I felt such elation at the concept of Morey's dancing around the throne of God. I was so thankful that I had been given the opportunity to know him even if it were for such a short time.

While preparing for the upcoming services, Dee called and said that she would like to have one of the pictures that I had taken as they wanted a current picture of his hair.

I will forever be grateful that Dee allowed me the blessing of her son. He was and still is an influence in my life.

God does have a plan and I love being a part of it.

NINETEEN
Satan is a Liar

John 8:44—You belong to your father, the devil, and you want to carry out your father's desire. He was a murderer from the beginning, not holding to the truth, for there is no truth in him. When he lies, he speaks his native language, for he is a liar and the father of lies. (NIV)

The dispatcher requested that I come into the station and talk with the Lieutenant. My not so favorite Lieutenant at that.

When I arrived at the station the Lieutenant told me that they had received a couple of calls from a female asking to talk with my husband about a police situation. She was told that he was not on duty. She told them she wanted to talk with him as she had heard that he was a Christian. After they again explained that Brandon did not work at night, the Lieutenant told her that Brandon's wife worked at night. Perhaps she could help. She then described her situation to the Command Officer. She felt a particular type of police officer was needed. I was asked to call the complainant on the phone to hear the details for myself.

I called the complainant who informed me that she was very concerned about her son. She said that she had just talked with her son, Jeff. He told her that he was very distraught. He said for several days he had been hearing a voice. This voice says to him, "Take a boning knife in your right hand and put it into your heart."

She told me that he had tried everything to get this voice to stop. He told her that he had brief reprieves but that he had been fighting this for about a week. Tonight he told her that he turned his radio on rather loud to drown out the voice. He then heard the voice coming from the radio. She said her dilemma was the fact that he was claiming that suicide might be his only way to rid himself of the voice.

Upon hearing this, I was absolutely stunned. Approximately two to four weeks earlier, my husband had come home from work relating the exact same set of facts from a call he had answered during the Day Shift. In this case, the young man involved had indeed taken a boning knife and stuck it into his heart.

He told friends that he was having this reoccurrence of the voice telling him to kill himself in that manner. When they found him on the floor of his home, they found a Bible on his bed. He had called his friend and told him that he was now hearing this voice coming from his radio.

After receiving all of the information from Jeff's Mother, I went in to see my "favorite Lieutenant". I told him I could handle the call. Under the circumstances I would probably have to bypass police policy. His response, "I don't give a good *** damn how you handle it. Just do it and take him with you", pointing to my Sergeant.

We went to Jeff's residence. I knocked on the door and identified myself. A slight built man answered the door carrying a small suitcase. He said that he just had to get out of that apartment. I told him his mother had called. I had him repeat for me the facts describing his problem. He did so, very much as the Mother had relayed it to me.

I then asked him if he knew Jesus Christ as his personal Savior. He told me that he had accepted Jesus as his Savior once some time ago but that circumstances in his life had changed and he had forsaken his relationship with God. As I am asking this question, my Sergeant is looking at me as though I have just lost my mind. I just kept talking.

I asked Jeff if he believed that Jesus had more power than the enemy who was trying to coerce him to commit suicide. He said yes he believed but he just did not have the strength to fight the fight.

At this point, the Sergeant asked that we go to our vehicles as we were standing in the hallway of this apartment building. I put Jeff in my car and informed him that I would be taking him to the hospital. He would be evaluated and not have to be alone for the evening. As the Sergeant was approaching his car, he said to me, "You know I used to go to Church."

I said to him, "Couldn't hurt to start going again."

When I got into my car, I turned around and asked Jeff if he would like to give up the fight and allow Jesus to take up the battle with the enemy. Jeff responded with an enormous sigh and a resounding, "Yes."

I then inquired of him, "Would you like to pray and ask the Lord to take over, renew your life and be your Warrior."

Jeff said that he would and he repeated after me a simple prayer of renewing his life with Christ and requested that Christ lead him, guide him and fight his battles for him. I then transported Jeff to the hospital and called his Mother to report the outcome. She thanked me and said that she would be in town to visit him the following day.

I often wondered how Jeff responded to his recommitment to the Lord. I accepted the fact that it was not necessary for me to have that knowledge. My responsibility was to be obedient to God's leading in my own life. Several months later, Brandon and I entered church one Sunday morning. Jeff greeted us at the door. He introduced us to the woman he was with, his Mother. They both shared their gratitude that God would place Christian Officers on the department. For me, I was grateful for the people who prayed for Christian Officers.

I'm so humbled to have been a part of God's plan.

TWENTY

Show Me The Money

Ephesians 5:11—Have nothing to do with the fruitless deeds of darkness, but rather expose them. ¹²For it is shameful even to mention what the disobedient do in secret. ¹³But everything exposed by the light becomes visible. (NIV)

You all know that police officers are stereotyped according to their coffee stops. I am here to tell you, that even while sipping java, valuable information may be garnered.

One such evening, at the bewitching hour of midnight, two young ladies of the night came into the Howard Johnson with a well-dressed male. One of the females was black and the other white. The threesome ordered coffee and before you know it they were on their way out the door.

Very shortly thereafter, the dispatcher interrupted a final sip of my coffee, alerting cars that a man had been relieved of his wallet at a nearby motel. It contained $800. Coincidentally enough, this motel was right next door to the Howard Johnson. When a description was given of the two thieves, it matched perfectly "our" ladies of the night. We left immediately and within a block both females were picked up walking in opposite directions. I transported the young black female to the station and was met there by a vice detective. I asked if he would like my help in questioning her and he said that he would get a hold of me if needed.

Approximately two hours later, the detective called requesting my assistance. He briefed me regarding his questioning. He had been unable to obtain any form of admission or determine the whereabouts of the cash. They had been thoroughly searched during the booking procedure.

It certainly appeared to me that there had not been an opportunity for these ladies to stash the money prior to arrest. He informed me that the other suspect had already been booked and put in a cell.

After offering me this information he added, "She's all yours."

I went into the interrogation room and I took one look at this girl and said, "You stuffed that money, didn't you?"

She actually was looking much more green than black to me. Immediately she admitted that she had quickly stuffed half of the money into her vagina, after she was brought into the station. I told her that we would have to take her to the hospital. She asked if I would give her the opportunity to try to retrieve it first. I gave her the opportunity, which resulted in a negative outcome. I reported these findings to the detective and offered to transport her to the hospital.

This young ladies complexion was a deeper shade of green by the time we arrived at the hospital. She was examined and forceps were used to retrieve $400. This young girl had to be in a lot of pain as she had literally stuffed this money inside her without rolling it or smoothing it out in any way.

The second perpetrator was also brought to the hospital under the assumption that possibly she had done the same thing. The investigators had not been able to find her half of the money and she continually claimed that she hadn't received any of the money.

I had known this young female most of her life. As the years progressed, I would see her from time to time. Every occasion that I came in contact with her, I could see her demeanor getting harder and harder. I went into the exam room to talk with her before the Doctor arrived.

I talked with her about her pattern of living and questioned how she had arrived at this point. I felt so deeply the emotional hurt that she revealed in her face. She related that no one cared for her.

I knew that had not always been the case. I shared with her that Jesus did indeed care for her and I also cared and would be there for her if she would allow me. She cried and told me that she would call me if she felt inclined. She then told me that the exam was not going to show anything as she had flushed the money down the stool while at the police station. I told her that I would have to put that in the report and she would be charged. She said she didn't care as she knew she would be identified anyway.

I grieved over the fate of this young lady. I prayed many nights that God would intervene and show her how much He really loved her. She never did contact me again. I still pray that she will yield to His call.

God has a plan and I have been only a very small part of it.

TWENTY-ONE
I Wish I Had Handled It Differently

Romans 7:15—I do not understand what I do. For what I want to do I do not do, but what I hate I do. (NIV)

Even while working Juvenile and Investigations I had remarks directed toward me of a sexual nature. None of them seemed very consequential at the time. Guys would make remarks at roll call like, "Capt. I'd sure like to work with her." Like I had no name.

On the other hand I would also hear remarks indicating that the speaker did not want to work with me. My point is that wanted or unwanted, the result was rejection and a deeply disturbing feeling of desolation. Both circumstances harassing, but not necessarily demeaning to the point of my losing sleep.

In that framework of time, it was not unusual for sexual remarks to be made in the presence of a female. Because it was a common and ordinary practice, mentioning it was an exercise in futility. When I was to mention to a Command Officer that Officer so and so's mouth offended me, I was always told to grin and bear it, "Remember, what we have already been through to keep you on the department?" Of course any memory of my past treatment went a long way.

However, by the time I had reached the Night Shift, my peers pretty well knew whom I stood for. They also knew that I wanted to lead an above board life. Let me make it clear, that I did not always succeed. I still repent between steps. Having prefaced this chapter, I tell you of another harrowing experience.

Why is it that individuals of small stature seem to have the largest mouths and try so desperately to make themselves appear larger than life? In this case, Sgt. Samuels fit that description perfectly. He was a short, loud-mouthed individual and had absolutely two personalities. He was Mr. Pottymouth when he was in the presence of more than one person. He was Mr. Ordinary when he was talking with you one-on-one.

Almost nightly, Sergeant Samuels, fortunately he was not my Sergeant, would meet me in the hallway when I came to work. His line, if you care to call it that, was always the same, "Want to hold my hand, want a little kiss," and almost always he ended it with a line that I would not even print. He was not the least bit concerned about who was present to hear these obnoxious remarks.

In case, at this point, you wonder why I have not done *something* about this little weasel, I remind you that my "favorite Lieutenant." is the Commander of the Shift and his Captain is not much better than the Sergeant spewing the offensive words.

One night when the Sergeant came into roll call, he went to the front and got onto his podium. Now he is taller and brasher.

He announced he was offering a 12-pack of beer to any officer who was successful at catching a crook in the process of breaking into a building during the shift.

Immediately one of my smart aleck peers pointed out that this was not a fair incentive, as "Jane doesn't drink beer."

Sergeant Samuels announced to the entire roll call, "That's OK I have another award planned for Jane."

Without missing a beat I proclaimed, "Hey it's OK, I'll start drinking beer."

After roll call I headed to the basement to find and set up my squad car. Officer Osburne was in the basement. He came over to my car and said that it really disturbed him that the Sergeant talked to me that way. I expressed my displeasure also and added that I had told him so, in the past, but to no avail. Officer Osburne asked me if I would try to do something about it officially.

I kindly explained to Officer Osburne that I had made inquiries with attorneys in the past and had been told that all of my complaints were too vague. I had been advised that pursuing this further would only hurt me and get me nowhere. Thus I told Officer Osburne that I had made a commitment to myself to "consider the source" and not take it personally.

For the next couple of months, I noticed that I seldom ever had a cover car unless the neighboring district car was available. By way of policy, if a district car was not sent to cover, a Sergeant was normally sent. I started to notice that when the Sergeant cars were called on; they answered and left the appearance that they were coming to cover me but they never showed up. It also started to register with me that while in the station neither Sergeant would speak to me.

At first, I appreciated the fact. I did not have to listen to the same harassing lines night after night. A few times, I went to dispatched calls that left me feeling very vulnerable. After I shared this with my fellow officers, they came whether dispatched or not, *if* they were available.

Two or three months went by and one evening I was dispatched to a Burglary in Progress on the North side of town. Sergeant Fred was sent to cover me. I arrived on the scene and reported that the back door was open to the business.

The owners of the business came and Sgt. Fred was not there. I requested permission to enter the building with the owners. Permission was granted. After we went into the building, another officer arrived to aid in checking out the surroundings, inside and out, for a possible burglar. Sergeant Fred never did show up.

After completing the report, I requested to meet Sergeant Fred in the parking lot of the business. He acknowledged and did show up there about 15 minutes later.

When I pulled up along side his car I said, "Hey, what the hell is going on? Neither you nor your Sergeant friend have shown up to cover me at a call for several months and I would like to know why?"

His reply knocked me right off my pins, "Well I'd like to know why you would file a sexual harassment suit against Sergeant Samuels and myself? We have just been waiting to get the official paperwork."

Even in my dumfounded state I responded, "Not that you don't deserve it, but who told you that?"

He then told me that quite some time ago he and Sergeant Samuels were called into "my favorite Lieutenant's" office and informed that I had filed this suit and so they should lay off the remarks, innuendos, etc.

I informed Sergeant Fred, in no uncertain terms, that I had not filed any sexual harassment suit nor had I ever threatened to. (I'm also certain that my language did not enhance my testimony).

I then drove straight to the police station where I approached Sergeant Samuels and I said to him, "I am absolutely not soliciting any of your foul remarks but I want you to know that I did not file any sexual harassment suit and I would appreciate from now on if you would cover my calls like you are supposed to." I turned around and walked out of the building and went back into service.

It was demeaning enough to listen to the nasty remarks but even more disturbing to be accused of following up on it, as I probably should have. I later found out that Officer Osburne had confronted "my favorite Lt." with this situation and he had chosen to handle it by lying to the Sergeants. And I am expected to respect this guy not only by department standards but also by God's.

I was failing this test but God had a plan and I was smack dab in the middle of it.

TWENTY-TWO
The Good Times

Ecclesiastes 3:12-13—I know that there is nothing better for men than to be happy and do good while they live, that everyone may eat and drink, and find satisfaction in all his toil-this is the gift of God. (NIV)

The work was at times stressful, like watching a four year old on a trapeze wire. Not thinking the toddler would fall off but rather that the wire would break.

The system of law enforcement is, in my opinion, fragile. That is why it cannot possibly work without the God given authority placed into reality, from the beginning of time. God placed government, and the authority of each government, under certain guidelines. God strictly monitors those guidelines. Therefore, he orchestrates their enforcement.

As an officer on the street, I watched the outcome of that orchestration many times.

I would then go to dinner or coffee with the troops and hear how *we* did this or how *they* accomplished the outcome. For my part, while en-route to coffee or dinner, I would be thanking and praising God that *we* were brought through that situation without anyone visiting the hospital by way of ambulance.

Needless to say, there were times when the sirens roared to our location and did transport downed officers to the ER.

Even on those occasions, I prayed that God would intervene and hasten the healing process without leaving the officer disabled or bedridden. I was always in awe at the end result, God's answer to prayer. I witnessed vehicle accidents, cancers, and knee and shoulder injuries and watched how God worked in the lives to heal both physically and spiritually.

Many times, I felt fortunate to be a female officer who loved God and had the privilege to pray for and lift up my peers as they went on hazardous calls.

Many nights, I would answer 4 or 5 calls while others handled 10 or 12. I thought often that while I was simply cruising my district I could at least be interceding for those on the front line. There were occasions when a call would be dispatched that involved the use of a deadly weapon.

If I was sent as one of the responding officers, it was a given that I would pray the entire length of the trip to the specified location. If I was not one of the responding officers, I made it a point to pray not only until they arrived but until they went 10:08 from the call. When the shift was over and the troops were emptying their cars of all the equipment used in their days work, I would hear one or two remark that they knew and were grateful that I was praying for them.

It became rewarding to know that while I was patrolling on one side of town I could offer protection of a Mighty God to those on the other side of town.

The good times included many nights of slow time when there were few calls. The hours were some time covered by talking with a fellow officer car to car. This was one of the sanity breaks when we could share with each other. We could talk about our families. We could speak of children who were doing well in school and sports. We could converse of family loyalty and encourage each other when we were experiencing stress of any kind. We could relate to similar problems created by the hours of the job. We became like family.

When a loyal fellow officer was transferred or bid off the shift it was like a family member moving away. Although you might see them between shifts, the camaraderie that was present while working side by side was now replaced by another face.

Food seems to be the ultimate provider of comfort. Our "group" had the incredible fortune to have a member whose parents ran "The Spaghetti Farm." These parents were the most supportive team that a night shift could ever hope to have. They allowed us to accompany their son into their establishment in the middle of the night and create great concoctions to eat. We grew to love the leftovers from the previous day's specials and even more, we loved the solitude of being able to eat without the public interrupting to recite the story of their great uncles mistreatment by the police.

In this place we were in a relaxing atmosphere free from the scrutiny of both the good and bad public. We may have had to warm up or cook our own but we could talk and laugh as loud as we wanted.

We had a tradition while I worked the night shift. Occasionally, without warning the majority of the shift might show up at your house for breakfast. The officer (without his knowledge) that was hosting this breakfast event went home as though he were headed to the pillow like he did every morning.

But...guess again. The rest of the crew made a stop at the grocery store and picked up a couple dozen eggs, four or five loaves of bread, bacon, sausage, juice and a few Danish. Inevitably, the host officer would have to drag himself out of bed and rummage around to find enough frying pans and other vital tools to cook for 12 to 15 hungry guys.

Of course we ate lightly during the night in order to accommodate a mega-breakfast. Well at least some of us ate lightly. It is an awesome, frightening experience to see this many guys in one kitchen. At my home, I try to run the guys out of the kitchen unless it is clean up time. After the plates are filled, it is a great time to trade war stories. They usually start with the most recent and before you know it, we are talking about 1972, or any year earlier.

Laughter is the main ingredient of this power breakfast and no one is ever disappointed. By about 11 AM or noon, the clean up, which usually includes scrubbing the floor, begins so we all can head for our own homes to try to make up for the four or five hours of sleep we have now already missed.

Just for the record, I don't think it was ever considered an honor to be the recipient host of these occasions. I transferred off the shift thinking that I had totally escaped this honor. Two weeks into the day shift, I was lavishing in the "sleeping in phase" of my day when I was wakened by the phone, which sounded like the defense siren was sitting on my nightstand. My first inclination was, "don't answer it."

However, the decibels appeared to becoming greater and I already couldn't stand the sound. So I answered with a very grumpy, "*Hello.*"

The replaying voice very simply said, "Hey–better get up, the night shift is having breakfast at your house this morning."

There was no need to tell me twice. I knew that time was short and I didn't want to be standing in my nightshirt when they arrived. My husband worked the day shift so I called and invited him home for breakfast.

He said, "Are you nuts, I am not coming home to that mess. I'll wait until it is cleaned up."

I will forever be grateful to the faithful caller who warned me. Several dozen eggs, 5 loaves of bread and 5 dirty frying pans later we relived the nights activities and I felt a part of the night shift once again. Somehow, at breakfast, the differences of opinions of the night before melted away and everyone was in agreement that today was a new day and with enough sleep they could all return the following night to fight crime and/or evil.

One of the last nights I worked, as I was unloading my equipment, the "group" approached me. They said that they had made arrangements for us and some of their wives to leave the station go right to the airfield where we could promptly take a few lessons and then sky dive.

After the initial hint of outrageous fear, I thought, Wow—this could be fun.

I went to my husband's office and told him that we were planning this auspicious outing. Without uttering a sigh or skipping a breath, my otherwise accommodating husband said, "If you do, don't come home, as I have enough anxiety with your working the night shift."

End of discussion and while the rest were flying through the air with the greatest of ease, I was snoozing soundly in my cozy bed. Of course, the next shift's discussion was ladened with over exaggerations of the previous day's activities. However, my marriage was worth saving.

I transferred to the School Liaison Program in 1986. For me, this was the end of an occupational era. I had survived the night shift because God placed honorable men there to train and guide me. I am forever grateful to them and to God who orchestrates a plan and uses us to carry it out.

TWENTY-THREE
Back in School Again

2 Timothy 2:15— Study and be eager and do your utmost to present yourself to God approved (tested by trial), a workman who has no cause to be ashamed, correctly analyzing and accurately dividing [rightly handling and skillfully teaching] the Word of Truth. (AMP)

Who would have thought that I would ever answer the morning bell at school—ever again? I, for one, never dreamed that I would again be wandering the halls of high school. Heaven only knows, I didn't like it when I roamed those corridors as a student. I will admit this was entirely a different set of circumstances.

I wanted to do my very best to fulfill the expectations of the Police School Liaison Officer. The Liaison Officer's responsibilities were to allow youth to become acquainted with law enforcement in a positive way and not always as handcuffed occupants of the rear seat of a squad car.

As I entered the high school that first morning, my mind immediately went to my first day of school at age 15.

I remembered vividly the insecurities of the teen years. I was reminded of the hurt that accompanies words whispered among peers. I watched as groups met in every corner of the corridors and locker areas. I witnessed shyness and aggressiveness within 20 feet of one another. Arrogance and inferiority were walking elbow to elbow down the hall. I knew that I was going to enjoy relating to the youth.

Orientation to the education element went without a hitch. I had, in the past, been to many of the city schools to give talks and conduct interviews of students involved or witnesses to crimes. Always I was impressed with the professionalism of the staff of individual schools and thus I was thrilled to have the opportunity to work out of one of the four high schools in our city.

In my estimation I had acquired the school that appeared to have the least problems. I was assigned to an office in the high school and was also responsible for the middle school and 11 elementary feeder schools. I found that I liked and clicked well with the supervisory staff. I became acquainted gradually and determined immediately those who were kindred spirits. I developed an immediate loyalty to the school.

I was succeeding a male officer who was abundantly appreciated. I was informed repeatedly that he was going to be missed. This officer and I were really good friends and so it was easy to reply, on these occasions, that it appeared more than obvious that he and I were not at all similar but that I would take up where he left off—but in different arenas.

In order to perform this assignment and maintain a good family life required that the week be instilled with an additional 20 hours.

I might as well break it to you. This did not happen. As a liaison officer, I was expected to work all the basketball games, football games, home wrestling meets, and any number of other activities held on school property.

Our daughter was in fourth grade at the time and in order to see her a few hours a day, I took her to school activities and she learned to be a part of them. She was cheering for the basketball team before she knew the first thing about the sport. When she wasn't watching the games, faculty members were entertaining her.

I gradually learned to appreciate all the extra-curricular activities, as it became the outlet to get to know the students. I have always had a great deal of care and compassion for teens. I became overwhelmingly fond of many of the students. Oddly enough I was not influenced by offences that may or may not have been committed by them. In other words, it didn't make any difference the caliber; God had given me a love for these teens.

There was a particular young man; I will call Terry who was a part of the "Behavior Disorder" classrooms. He had a very difficult task just remaining a civilized member of the society. The classroom teachers dealt with his lack of behavior to the extent they were able. He was very disruptive and spent as much time in the Assistant Principal's office as he did in the classroom.

Occasionally his behavior was such that the Assistant Principal would escort him to my office in order that I might acquaint him with the criminal code, regarding assault, theft and other broken laws that are too numerous to mention.

On one of these incidents, I was explaining to Terry that he was breaking the law and consequently I would have to prepare a report including all the details of the particular crime to be forwarded to the Juvenile Justice System.

Terry very calmly replied to my explanation, "Did you know that I have the power to place a curse on you? I have accomplished this with almost all of my behavior disorder teachers."

With just as much serenity, I replied, "Hey pal, you may or may not have succeeded in your previous placement of curses but of one thing I can guarantee, you will not accomplish a thing with me, as I serve the Lord Jesus Christ and He protects me from such evil causes." This statement ended our interview and the paperwork went forward without any more comment.

Approximately 1 year later Terry had a very "heard all over the first floor" outburst in the Assistant Principal's office. I was summoned but Terry had left the office after slamming numerous doors prior to my arrival. The Assistant Principal informed me, that Terry had said he was going to return with a gun to shoot him. Bright and early this same fall morning, as I entered the building, I was met by a frantic student. This student told me a story about a fellow pupil who had stolen a handgun from his parent's house and had hidden it at a specified location. I assured this student that I would look into the story and ascertain whether there was any substance of truth. I further explained that it might be simply a plea for attention.

I immediately knew, although this was not the student who had allegedly stolen the weapon from his parent, that Terry and the thief student were pals. Thus, I knew that Terry did indeed have access to a gun. I relayed this report to the Assistant Principal and told him that I would be leaving in an attempt to find Terry. The Assistant Principal, asked if he could go with me. I agreed and we hurried to my squad car.

On our way out of the parking lot, I informed the Communications Center of the situation and she dispatched another car to the area.

Just as I thought, Terry was headed straight for the address where I had been told the gun had been hidden. Upon approaching him, I asked him to get into the car in order that we might visit about the circumstances and attempt to make some sense of what had just taken place. As he entered the back seat of my car, I radioed for the patrol car to meet me at the high school to transport a young man to juvenile detention.

When Terry heard the transmission, he said, "It is a good thing I like you Mrs. A or you would be in big trouble."

I was then and still am convinced that he didn't like me but he knew that the voodoo that he used with others was useless when dealing with my God.

In order for you the reader to get a good grip on the dynamics involved with my position, I must tell you that my "favorite Lieutenant" (from nights) was now my "favorite Captain" and had been transferred to head up the Professional Standard Division, which is responsible for the Liaison Officers.

In November of 1987 the Crime Analyst for our police department called me and asked if I was aware or had come in contact with any alleged cult activities at the high school.

I reported that we had several girls in the school that dressed in all black, painted their faces a faint white and wore ruby red lipstick. I also informed him that we had heard rumors about an animal's heart that had been thrown from a school bus onto a car in the school parking lot.

I related that the county was investigating this as the bus had been from a school located in the county and they had already been advised of the circumstances and were actively pursuing it. I further expounded that we had heard many rumors, like the fact that there had been blood smeared on the wall of the corridor outside the music room.

Upon interviewing students and teachers, I could not find anyone who had actually seen this. I did tell the Crime Analyst that should we come up with information substantiating any of these facts, that I would dictate on it and take action.

In December 1987 my now "favorite Captain" made several inquiries of my Lieutenant regarding what I was doing about the cult activities at the high school. The Lieutenant called me to see if I had any additional feedback to add to my previous suspicions. I told him that I could only relate that we had asked the girls dressed in black if they belonged to a group called the "Black Widows" as we had been informed. They said that they only wore black to emulate a German Rock group.

I had heard rumors that there was to be a ritual sacrifice and the victim would be a blond haired, blue-eyed girl. One of the stories included the fact that she was a cheerleader. Consequently I called one of the girls into my office that fit the description of the "sacrifice victim."

She said yes she was getting threatening phone calls. The caller was muffled and he just said that he was "Jason."

There was no actual threat but with the rumors being circulated, the teens added the rest. I inquired of her if there were other victims that she knew of and I was told of a couple more girls. I called them into my office and talked with them. They too related that they had been receiving strange phone calls but could not tell me what was said to them.

In an effort to squelch the fear, I arranged for phone taps to be attached to their lines by the phone company for a couple of weeks. These produced nothing. An information report was made and the circumstances dictated.

A week or so later, my Lieutenant called and said that the Captain had reviewed my report and was now very concerned that I had not followed through on this situation.

The Captain suggested that I was covering up something and thought that it had something to do with the church that I attended. The Lieutenant asked his Captain why in the world he would make this particular accusation. The Captain informed him that he had heard that our church had a very active youth group and written on the marquee at our church were the words, "The Blood." I don't think it takes much explanation to the reader what that sign meant.

At the beginning of the following month, the Captain contacted the Lieutenant and said that he felt that it was time for us to give the news media some answers as they had been asking a lot of questions about this "cult activity."

The Lieutenant spoke with me and I pleaded with him not to allow this to happen as we had just been hearing rumors and had not been able to substantiate anything. I also told him that the school would take a ton of criticizing if this occurred.

At this point, we now had about 13 girls dressing in black and a couple of young men. The Assistant Principal asked if I would talk with the girls and inform them that although they were within the school guidelines to dress this way that they might like to discontinue the all black due to the hostility that had been directed toward them due to the rumors.

While I had them in my office, I again asked them if they were now involved in or had they ever been involved in a group associated with Satanism. One of the girls looked me square in the eye and said, "Mrs. A, we are Christian girls."

I asked if they all agreed to this description. They all said that they did. Thus I told them that the Bible said that if they were Christians that they could easily be identified by simply confessing with their mouths that Jesus is Lord. So, I said, "We will start with you and go around the room and all I need you to say is that Jesus is Lord."

Not one of them would do so. I reiterated that it would probably be best to discontinue dressing in all black as the dress code said that if clothing was a disruption to the school setting that it would have to be addressed. The following day all but one of them came to school in regular attire.

A couple of days later, I awoke to the following headlines in the City newspaper: NO SUBSTANCE TO EAST CULT RUMORS.

The staff at the high school was livid and felt that I had to have been a participant in engineering this article. The articles continued in the paper for about three days. By the time the tempers cooled down at the high school so did the subject of Satanic Cults.

See Pages 116 – 118

Did I think that there was genuine cult activity occurring? Of course I did. Believing that something is happening and proof of it are two very different things.

On one occasion another officer and I found what appeared to be the remains of a worship site on a teacher's property. The site was arranged in the shape of a pentagram and there were log stools set at the points of the star. There was evidence of a fire also.

The problem with this knowledge was that we were trespassing when we found it and therefore could not use it as evidence. And, if we could have used it, to what end ?

Near the end of the school year, several teachers approached me. Three or four instructors surrounded me in the hallway. They revealed they had overheard students plotting a large skip day that specific day.

A short time later, while in the mailroom, I was circled by another four or five teachers and informed they had information that a skip day had been orchestrated. They further related the rumor there was going to be a very large keg party at the Missouri River.

»

I contacted my fellow Liaison Officers and requested their help in addressing this problem. I then contacted my immediate command and explained the situation to him. Officer McGee, and I would be checking for the whereabouts of this abundant party of students. We had over 100 absences.

Officer McGee and I searched the area of the River from the Iowa side for quite some time. From the Iowa side, we did in fact, observe several individuals on the beach area of the Nebraska side. It was impossible to determine with the naked eye if these were adults or teens. Furthermore, if they were youths, were they students from our high school?

Officer McGee and I made a quick trip to headquarters in order to retrieve a pair of binoculars. While I was picking up the binoculars, the head of the Identifications Division was in the equipment area and he offered a 1000 mm camera that would take good pictures at that range.

We returned to the site and viewed the area through binoculars.

There were approx. 25 to 40 young people on the beach area. I could not see clear enough to determine if there were any beer cans. There was no beer keg in site. While looking at this scene, I observed a man in a green uniform, quite similar to the Lakota County Deputies uniforms.

He walked onto the beach and talked with several of the youths. He then left the area. Officer McGee and I then drove to the South Border City, Nebraska side of the river and drove the roadway that leads to the beachfront. There, we found several cars with Border City license plates. We noted the plate numbers in order to address the truancy issue.

After returning to the Police Station, I called South Border City, Chief Gene Clarkson to inquire about the individual wearing the green uniform that we had seen on the beach. He told me that he believed it was probably a conservation officer as they wore green uniforms.

The following morning my immediate command officer called to make me aware of the fact that "my favorite" Captain was extremely unhappy with me for taking pictures at the River when it regarded truancy which was none of my concern. The Captain said that a parent had called the Chief of Police complaining that I should have done something. The Captain added, "And furthermore, where is the police report?"

Now I don't mind telling you that I was very concerned. I was informed that this was not a police related problem and none of my concern. In the next breath, I was told that I should have made a police report. In my reasoning, I would have made a police report if I had been able to establish that alcohol had been a part of the scenario.

I had been unable to do this. I did not physically go to the beach area, as we have no jurisdiction in Nebraska. I had attempted to contact Lakota City dispatch to ascertain who might have been checking on this party but they were unable to furnish me with this information.

Two days pass and I was contacted by my police supervisor and told that the Captain wants a written report in regard to the truancy issue on the river. This report was prepared and dictated upon.

At the same time, the Captain had requested the Sergeant submit a written memo expressing his opinion of my actions. The Sergeant did inform me of this request and he also assured me that he had already made it verbally clear to the Captain that he approved of my actions. He would put the same report in writing.

I was told that when the Captain received this written assignment that he became red in the face, that the veins on his neck protruded and he told the Sergeant, "You will rewrite this assessment." And with that said, he threw the paperwork at him.

The Sergeant replied that he would take whatever suspension was appropriate but that he had no intention of changing the substance of his report. Very bravely he said, "This issue would not exist except that her name is Jane."

At the same time, the Captain told the Sergeant, "She is completely incompetent."

He accused my Sergeant of an inability to be fair and impartial and threatened to transfer him back to the Uniform Shift. The Sergeant offered to go back to Uniform if that was his true belief. I thanked God for a Sergeant that was willing to follow his principles and not be bullied into writing what he did not believe to be true. I also asked God to protect him as he took a stand.

With this information, I was certain that the "skip day" issue had been put to rest. By this time I felt the attempt to completely undermine my position with the school was fairly close to complete. I felt humiliated that, in a city where there was so much more serious crime, that I would be scrutinized for days in regard to high school children skipping school. And, it had already been pointed out to me that this issue was none of my concern as a police officer.

The end of April, I received a call at the end of the school day from Officer ML of the Major Offender Team (aka Vice Squad). He informed me that they had planted an undercover person in our school. He told me the name of the student and the student that they were after. I then informed ML that I had heard rumors about this suspect, connecting him to drugs. I also told ML that I did, in fact, know the undercover person. Officer ML notified me that the reason for his call was that he thought a school official should be informed of this.

School had already been dismissed for this day so I proceeded to do my parking lot duties and determined that I would address the facts with the administration the following day.

The next day, I approached the Assistant Principal whom I trusted most to keep a confidence. I told him the entire scenario. He immediately informed me that he absolutely could not keep this from the building Principal. I begged and pleaded with him and he simply said that the risk was too great not to inform the Principal sighting examples of situations that could occur. I had no control of the transfer of information. The Principal was told of the circumstances.

Two days later I received a call from my faithful Sergeant. He said that the Chief of Police had just visited him. The Chief ranted and raved about a phone call that he had just completed with the Superintendent of schools.

The Chief was at the pinnacle of a temper tantrum and he said, "What the f**k do you know about that East High Liaison Officer?" Sergeant P then told me that they were not aware of the drug investigation going on at the high school. The Sergeant invited me, at the Chief's request, to a meeting in the Chief's office for that afternoon.

After receiving the unwelcome invitation, I bounced all the previous accusations around in my head. Not just the "skip day" thing but also the years of mental, emotional and verbal abuse. I contemplated refusing to meet with them without an attorney present. I then thought perhaps that was reaching the very edge of paranoia so I opted calling our Association President and requesting that he just sit in on this meeting. He agreed to meet me at the Chief's office that afternoon.

Now keep in mind that this is not my first day on this job. Furthermore, I was born before noon of this particular day. So, when I tell you that I went and purchased a very small tape recorder to have a permanent record of the substance of this meeting, you will not be surprised, right?

Upon entering the Chief's office, with Officer MH, President of our Police Association at my side, the Assistant Chief looked at me and snarled, "what is he doing here?' At which I replied, "I would like someone here to be able to recite both sides of this meeting. We have present in the room, Asst. Chief Coffee, my "favorite Captain", Sergeant P, Officer MH and myself.

Imagine the unenthusiastic emotion I experienced when the first topic of this meeting was–Yep, you guessed it–"skip day."

Sgt. P was asked if he had Officer MGee's dictation about the day in question. Approximately ½ hour was spent discussing this "party" and my irresponsibility in regard to not having done something. "Imagine our liability if something had happened to one of those kids."

My thought, "Now all of the sudden this was within the realm of police responsibility." What I said was–nothing. At one point, my "favorite Captain" tells me that he had called Chief Clarkson and had been informed that the conservation officers did not wear green uniforms but that they did indeed wear brown.

His point was made very bluntly, insinuating that I had lied in my written report. Without hesitation I retorted that I too had spoken with Chief Clarkson and he had absolutely told me that the conservation officer's uniform was green. I also offered to get Chief Clarkson on the speakerphone to verify the truth. After receiving my reply, my "favorite Captain" inserted that perhaps he had spoken with the South Border City Dispatcher and not Chief Clarkson.

The rest of our meeting was spent talking about the "drug investigation" at our High School. The conversation began by the Captain referencing a conversation that I had with Officer ML regarding a drug issue and how badly I had compromised that investigation. He said that he had a written statement on his desk from Officer ML relating the contents of his conversation with you. In this statement Officer ML apparently said that he had cautioned you about the confidentiality of this investigation and that no one was to know about it.

He indicated that I was the school official that he was making aware of the circumstances. I asked if Officer ML could be summoned to be present in order that I might address this statement with him. Asst. Chief C shouted, "No, this is about you, not Officer ML."

With an extreme amount of calm that had to have fallen on me from the Holy Spirit, I said, "These facts that you present are simply not true and I reiterated my version of our conversation."

My "preferred Captain" just kept saying that I had jeopardized a drug investigation and brought embarrassment to the Chief's office because when the School Superintendent phoned him to check it out, the Chief was totally unaware of the facts of this investigation. The Chief then said that he checked with the Captain of the Major Offender team and that Captain was unaware of this investigation also.

I made attempts to defend myself with this information, saying that it was not my investigation and not my responsibility to inform the Command of this particular case.

When this meeting was coming to an end, I was ordered to make a written report of my conversation with Officer ML. I was also ordered to resubmit a report in regard to the "skip day."

They claimed never to have seen the official report. Then I was told that after reading these reports, they would *determine* what to do with me.

I was asked by the Captain, "Do you have any further questions?"

I explained that I was puzzled why I could not ask for the other Liaison Officer and Office ML to participate in this meeting, as they also were involved. My "beloved Captain" bellowed, as he pounded his desk, "Because this is about *you.*"

I left this office in utter defeat. I could not determine in my own thinking whether I had done anything wrong or if I was totally right. The one thing I knew for sure either way, I was looked upon as a wrong, bad person. I had so much love in my heart for people and particularly for the East High students and faculty that I was crushed to think that anyone would suspect that I would take or not take action to protect them.

Several times in the following weeks, I asked my Sergeant and my Lieutenant if the Assistant Chief or the Captain had *determined* my fate in regard to the two incidents.

I remained distressed by the fact that I had been referred to as completely incompetent. I was further devastated at being described as an officer who would purposely jeopardize a drug investigation especially since I had lobbied at length to get someone to address the drug use by the students in our building.

»

Two months later after a meeting of the Professional Standards Division, I asked Lieutenant B if he would inquire of the Assistant Chief on my behalf regarding my status and possibility of a pending suspension. I explained that I felt this had been hanging over my head long enough.

Lieutenant B called me two days later and relayed to me the following quote, "No, I have no intention of giving her any response. And the situation will remain in my bottom drawer unless or until I need it."

You might guess that this was less than assurance for me. I was once again requesting that the Holy Spirit anoint me with His Peace.

The three years that I spent in the School Liaison Program were the most satisfying for me. I always had a great deal of love and understanding for teenagers. I suffered from an extreme lack of confidence during my own teen years. Therefore, I made a concentrated effort to address students with the same respect and honor that I wanted to receive from them. Consequently I made some life long friends there, both from the faculty sector as well as from the student population.

As my third year approached, the high school principal sent a letter to the Chief of Police requesting that I be able to retain the position for another year. Mr. D, the principal was already aware of the fact the other two high schools had been allowed to keep their liaison officers for an additional year. Mr. D was given an immediate no with the explanation that Police Policy stated that the position was strictly written for a three year term in order that the officer not get out of touch with mainstream police work.

Because the circumstances were so drastically unfair compared to the treatment of others on the department, I filed an official grievance. This procedure takes quite some time and all steps were denied by the administration to the point of having to go to arbitration. At this point in the process, the arbitrator ruled that the police policy distinctly set out the time span and thus I was subject to that policy. Although the situation with the other two liaison officers was testified to in the hearings, it was never mentioned in the arbitrator's findings. Again, I was hurt, disappointed and felt discarded by the system.

A few months later, our family moved to an acreage, on the outskirts of town. This move required a lot more at-home time, which would not have been available had I still been assigned to the school. Gardening, mowing, and transporting a junior high daughter to a neighboring town for school activities took a great deal of time. It became immediately apparent to me that God had a plan and I tried desperately to mess it up.

TWENTY-FOUR
Double Standards

Acts 10:34—Then Peter began to speak: "I now realize how true it is that God does not show favoritism. (NIV)

January 26, 1989 after finishing preliminary responsibilities at the high school, I headed for the Professional Standards office at headquarters. We (the Liaison Officers and our Command) met there on Fridays and discussed the week's occurrences and were given reports to be followed up for the following week. Then, as a group we went to coffee.

On this occasion, the group had left the building to attend coffee prior to my finishing my paperwork. Upon completion, ten minutes later, I proceeded to the Holiday Inn Coffee Shop. At the intersection of W 4th and Cook Streets a man driving a custom van made an abrupt left turn in front of me.

The impact of our vehicles sounded to me like two freight trains hitting head on. I was quite shaken and had neck pain thus a Personal Injury Accident report was made. I missed one half day's work.

A month later, my Lieutenant called saying that he had been informed by the Assistant Chief of Police that I was to dictate a supplementary report giving an explanation regarding why I was at W 4th & Cook Streets on January 26 when my school assignment was on the other side of town. Lieutenant B explained the situation to the Assistant Chief and he still insisted on a written report.

Although this did not come as a surprise to me, I did make note in my subconscious that on previous accident occasions, I had never been asked to give an account for my whereabouts nor did I know anyone else on our department who had.

I did comply and made a supplementary report to the initial accident report. At the same time, I determined to conduct a small investigation of my own to see if others were required to write supplementary reports upon the occurrence of an accident.

My findings were rather remarkable, at least to my way of thinking. My memory served me well. I had remembered my favorite Captain having an accident a short time prior. I went to the Record Room and sure enough at 10:00 PM on 12/23/1988 he had indeed been in an accident with a city vehicle. His vehicle struck a parked car in the parking lot of the local College. After finding the original report, I sought a supplementary report but was told by records personnel that short form accident reports did not require supplementary reports.

Checking further, I found that Assistant Chief Coffee had also been involved in an accident the previous year. This accident also involved the Chief's striking a parked vehicle.

The accident was made on a short form accident report (which indicated that the damage was under $500). Of course I attempted to read the supplementary report and found (not at all to my surprise) that there was no supplementary report. Since I had spent so much time in investigations, I took the case of the missing report one step further and checked the auto body shop that repaired our vehicles and lo and behold I found the written receipt for the repair of the Assistant Chief's vehicle. The damage totaled $875.

I was having so much success with my investigation. I thought that perhaps I should check on the top dog. So I went to the daily log as I had heard that he had two accidents since his appointment as Chief of our department.

The most recent accident, which I had been told, by the driver of the other vehicle, had occurred at North High School was not recorded at all. There was no written report involving this accident. I had also been informed that the Chief had an accident in 1983.

I found the accident listed on the log and the names of the officers who took the report. Upon looking for the accident on microfilm, I was told that any information regarding that report had been purged. The Lieutenant in charge of the day shift at the time told me that a long form report had been taken at the scene as the damage was well over $500. The following day he was ordered by the Chief to put it on a short form. The Lieutenant told me that he had checked on the report a year later and it was totally purged from the system.

These stories I relate to you for one reason only. This has nothing to do with the fact that I was a female. In the months and years that preceded these sets of circumstances and in the years since, I have listened to many other officers both male and female relate similar facts in their dealings with command. This has everything to do with the fact that the uppermost command was not expected to follow the rules. And, if there were no rules regarding their desires, they invented them.

All of this led to additional resentment and complete disrespect and contempt for the authority of their offices. I had already entirely lost respect for them as human beings.

Let's face it, I very naively thought that life was fair and that integrity was still a virtue that was alive and active in our society. One scenario at a time, I came to understand that honor, truth and uprightness were words utilized but the definitions were unfamiliar to the upper echelon.

Was I entitled to the bitterness, resentment, contempt that I felt for these people? Perhaps on a worldly level but God's level required a whole different outlook of which I was not presently utilizing but God had a plan and I would soon learn of it.

TWENTY-FIVE

Back on the Street Again

1 Samuel 15:22---Samuel replied, "What is more pleasing to the LORD: your burnt offerings and sacrifices or your obedience to his voice? Obedience is far better than sacrifice. (NLT)

Willie Nelson sings the song, "Back on the Road Again." The same tune echoed in my brain in June of 1989, which found me in uniform, on the street again. Another transition under way. After having proven myself to the schools, I was now back in to the familiar roll call room.

It seems that one always has to claim their territory and make it known what you will and will not tolerate. In many occupations, and police shift work was not excluded, seniority plays an important role. Therefore it was vital that I determine right off the get go, who sat in which seat at roll call and who possessed more seniority than I.

The next most important task was to determine by the above facts, which car I might be entitled to drive. All these crucial facts were not resolved in one shift. It took two or three to put together who sat where and who drove what. When all of these specifics became crystal clear, I could concern myself with districts and the likelihood of being assigned one, which I might actually desire. I thought perhaps, after my prior experiences that the best way to keep from gaining a district that I liked or disliked would be solved best by just keeping my mouth shut. A monumental undertaking for me.

This time it worked. I was assigned to a district that I was very familiar with and where I knew a great deal of the businesses and their owners.

It would seem that answering calls in your own district and minding your own business should be an easy task and by doing so, a shift would go by fairly quickly. However, your own district is not the only factor to take into consideration. One of the essentials that I learned working the night shift was the fact that the officers that work the districts neighboring yours were very important. All this came back to me in a flash after acclimating myself to D-6.

Great officers manned the districts adjoining mine. There was never a time when I couldn't count on them. Many days were strictly routine; alarms, traffic accidents, vandalism, abandoned vehicles, domestic disputes, and neighborhood squabbles. Occasionally a call would leave a lasting remembrance. I instantaneously recorded these in my memory bank of unforgettable occurrences.

One such memory involved a call received from a respectable motel complaining that they had a guest who turned out not to be too welcome. The report indicated that she was utilizing her room for the purpose of prostitution.

My Sergeant and I were dispatched to this location. After receiving written statements from witnesses, etc., we made our way to her room. She let us in the room and she was placed under arrest. While gathering up her belongings before transporting her to jail, it became quite apparent that she was interested in and possibly accomplished in witchcraft. She had many items of the craft; tarot cards, books on the subject, crystals, etc.

I led her to my squad car and placed her in the back seat. After starting the car, the radio started playing. My music of choice was Christian music and thus it filled the cars atmosphere..

The very moment the music started, my prisoner went absolutely wild. She started screaming, "Get me out of this car. I cannot be in the same car with this type of music."

Sgt. B who had just entered his vehicle, which was parked next to mine was looking over at the scene in my car with total astonishment. He got out of his car and said to me, "What did you say to her?"

I grinned one of those 'ear to ear' type smiles and said, "I have said nothing–yet."

While the Sgt. was standing there the female prisoner lay down on the back seat and started trying to kick out the window of the squad car. At the same time she is bellowing, "Turn that thing off, turn that radio off."

I turned around and said, "My car, my station."

In 19 years of law enforcement, I had been continually submitted to vile sites, smells, sounds, and language that would curl your hair. It felt so refreshing to say this was my music. This worshiped the God that I serve. I intended that it remain on my car radio until the day I retired.

For the 6 miles to the police station this prisoner kicked at the back window. As soon as the car was in the bay at the jail, the kicking stopped and she accompanied me without incident to the booking window. Obviously spiritual warfare is a powerful force no matter which side we are tackling it from. I determined to remember this fact in my future prayers.

The call that I describe to you now was one of those that elicited prayer from the moment that it left the dispatchers lips. I was told that a mentally challenged man was very distressed as he was having hallucinations or something indicating that Jesus was trying desperately to get a message to him.

My cover car was from the neighboring district and a wonderful person. However, he did not understand nor did he want to know anything about spiritual matters. He had voiced this to me on more than one occasion. I do not write this to be critical. He had a divine right to his free will and I did not fault him for it. I did however pray for him continually and I know that God has a plan for his life.

We both arrived at the call at approximately the same time. I asked him if he would interview the complainant and that I would talk with the young man with the visions. I knocked on the young man's apartment and he allowed me entrance. He immediately started telling me that he had recently been reading the Bible. He said that he had never been exposed to it nor it's teachings in the past. He claimed that he had been questioning (perhaps in prayer, although I do not know that) whether he should go so far as to acknowledge Christ and the fact that He had died for him. I then confronted him with the fact that we had been told that he was having hallucinations of some sort.

As I finished that statement, my Sergeant showed up, dismissing the doubting officer to answer another call. My Sergeant was also a Christian. The young man said that he was pondering the question of acceptance of Jesus when he looked at the door to his bedroom. He said that he saw the door of his bedroom covered with blood as though it were washing down the entire door. He said that it frightened him and that is why he called his friend who in turn called the police.

I asked him if this "vision" meant anything to him in a spiritual sense. It might be noted here that I would not have felt the freedom to ask this question if the other Officer had been present. He said that he thought possibly the Lord was showing him that Jesus died for his sins. He further thought that possibly if he acknowledged and accepted Him he could rest peacefully.

I asked him then if he would truly like to accept Jesus as His Savior and he said yes that he would. I prayed with this young man as Sergeant B held us both up in prayer. We left this call knowing that God indeed directs our paths and we were both thankful for it.

As we both announced to the dispatcher that we were 10:08 or back in service, she immediately dispatched us to another call. This call was explained to us as a possible suicide attempt. The details were that an elderly man had sent his caregiver to the store to pick up some groceries. The caregiver in turn called the police as she said that "Fred" (not correct name) was acting strangely to her. She said that he was giving her details, which would lead anyone to believe that his life was being finalized. She was told where his will was kept and how to contact next of kin.

When we arrived at the address given, a couple of men were visiting with him. I asked to talk with Fred alone and while doing so, Sgt. B took the men outside to see if they knew anything. They related that our complainant had also called them as they were acquaintances. They confirmed that he was completely depressed and that he had told them that he intended to take an excess of his pain medication, attempting to end his life. He was a cancer patient and was in extreme pain.

I asked Fred if it was his intention to take his life and he said that it was indeed. He said that he was all alone in the world. He expressed that his caregiver was essentially a stranger and did not personally care about him. He lamented that his spouse had passed away and he simply wanted to depart and go be with her.

I set about explaining that when no one else loved us and cared for us that Jesus was always there and could be counted on to comfort us. I asked him if he had ever heard the message of salvation or how Jesus died for us on the cross. He said that he never had. I asked if he would like to acknowledge Jesus as His Savior and ask Him to care and comfort him. Fred very gently and with great respect said that he did not want to do this instantly but would like to have a chance to think about it.

I told him that I would pray that God would reveal himself to him and we were on our way.

Needless to say I would have been exuberant if Fred had agreed to pray with me. I also know that God loved him and I asked God daily, as I traveled that district, to meet Fred where he was and to bring him peace and healing. I watched for his obituary in the paper for 4 or 5 years after that and never did see it. I pray that God healed him.

During the years that I worked days, I worked a neighboring district next to Officer Parker. For a few years my husband had been on the same shift with Officer Parker and they had coffee together and occasional dinner breaks. They became fairly close friends. Whenever Officer Parker and Brandon went on their breaks together, Brandon would come home in a very negative, pessimistic frame of mind.

After a while, I started to see a pattern form. I would say to Brandon, "I would appreciate it immensely if you would attempt to keep an upbeat mood after having breaks with Parker."

Now several years later I am the one working with Parker and having coffee and occasional lunches with him. After a pattern formed, now it was Brandon telling me to keep an optimistic attitude while I was having breaks with Parker. If I were to purposely pick a friend, it would not be Parker. We had two completely conflicting views on life, people, handling calls, and anything else one would like to mention. The only view that we held in common, or at least I thought, was physical fitness. I'm certainly not attempting to insinuate that I held myself to the letter of the fitness law, but at the very least, I wished that I had.

We started lifting weights and working together to achieve the goal of physical fitness. Of course, I was involved in many other goal setting achievements and would often miss a day here and there at the torture hour. Consequently we would have total disagreements in regard to priorities. Mine centered around Christ. I felt as though his centered around personal achievement.

Many hours during coffee and lunches we discussed both. Although I don't believe that I ever achieved the ultimate goal of convincing him that Jesus was *the* most precious friend. I did gain a great deal of respect for a man who held to his convictions and who was not critical of mine.

Parker's wife Jackie and I became good friends. I was continually overwhelmed with family values that they possess. I am grateful to them both for their willingness to include us so many times in their family setting. I continue to pray that Jesus becomes the center of their existence. We can often share our relationship with Jesus and in this case, I even know that Parker agreed but did not confess to that belief. I don't need to be the person to hear that confession, I only pray that someone hears them say "Jesus is Lord."

»

On a bleak Sunday morning as I patrolled my district, I was grumbling to the Lord about the fact that I had to work so many Sundays. I continued on for 20 or 30 miles carrying on about how I would prefer to be in church worshiping, singing to Him, and listening to His Word being preached. Before long, I was very depressed and I was having a very lonely pity party. A torrential rain had occurred the night before. I received a dispatched call to go to an address and talk with a lady in regard to mud that had washed onto her sidewalk from the neighboring yard.

When I arrived at the home, it was easy to locate the correct address, as the sidewalk approaching the house was just loaded with mud. I rang the doorbell and was met at the door by a slight framed, 8oish, white haired lady using a walker.

She was bordering on rage. She explained to me that every time the rains come, her sidewalk soon looks like her lawn, without the grass. I asked her if she had ever talked with her neighbors about the problem. I thought that perhaps some sort of terracing or planted shrubbery might solve the problem. She admitted that she had not talked with them.

After conversing about the situation for a short period of time, she started telling me how lonely she was. Since this was Sunday, I asked her if she was ever able to attend church on Sunday. She told me that at one time she had gone to church regularly but that people were not so inclined to pick her up since she had gotten slower and especially since she started to use a walker.

I asked if she ever listened to church services on the radio on Sunday morning or if she had an opportunity to listen to daily Christian radio. She informed me that she did not even know where to find a Christian radio program. Because she had a radio on the shelf right next to the couch, I offered to tune it in to one of the Christian radio stations. As I was dialing for the correct frequency, I asked her if she had every invited Christ to be her personal Savior. She told me that she had attended church almost her whole life but that she had never verbally done that although she had considered it a time or two. I asked her if she would like to include Him in her daily life. She simply beamed and said that she would love to.

Full uniform and all, I knelt at her feet and prayed with her to ask Jesus to forgive her sin, to accept Him as her personal Savior and Redeemer. I left her humble home repenting for my previous attitude and Praising God for the supreme opportunity to pray with this lovely lady.

Three weeks later, I was dispatched to the same address very early on a week day morning. The paperboy had called reporting that when he went to deliver her paper, her window shades were up approximately 3 inches. He noted that the window shades were always fully drawn when he delivered her paper and he was concerned. He had knocked on her door and had not received an answer.

Upon my arrival, I did not receive an answer to my ringing or knocking either. I called the fire department who helped me gain entrance to her home. This lovely lady had apparently died the night before. She was lying next to her walker, which was right in front of the television. I am so grateful to know that she had so willingly given her heart to Jesus just three weeks before.

»

Twenty-three years I had spent on the BCPD. As the final years were closing in, I was continually nagged by the resentment, hateful feelings I harbored toward my "not so favorite" Lt. and now Captain. Many times during prayer time I would feel the conviction of hanging onto such godless feelings. Every time I would have myself thoroughly convinced that this was the day I would finally forgive him, I would run into him in the hallway and he would make a snide remark to me. Or perhaps I would run into him in the command office and I would hear him berating a fellow officer.

Whenever this occurred, I simply collected another imaginary nail that I was saving to seal his coffin. By this time I had a whole peck of them.

One particular Sunday evening at our church service, our pastor preached on forgiveness. He talked a great deal about how unforgiveness created enormous bitterness and hindered health and subsequent healing. I made up my mind that I would go directly to "my favorite" Captain's office the following morning and verbally ask for his forgiveness.

The next morning I arrived at the station and "lo and behold" there in the command office was the Captain. As I approached the office, I overheard him belittling fellow officers in the presence of peers and the shift lieutenant.

The comments made did not remotely involve the handling of their jobs but were more personal in nature. I also recognized that his references were directed about officers that he had personal vendettas against. My instant reaction was the reverse of forgiveness. I turned around on a dime and stomped back to my squad car where I seethed until I was distracted by genuine police work. I justified my attitude by his complete lack of responsible supervisory attitudes and behavior.

Several weeks later on my day off, I was having lunch with a good friend. The chosen location for this lunch was an out of the way, not very popular spot. As we were eating and conversing, my friend started to share a story with me about her ex-husband who had been responsible for a great deal of pain in her life. She proceeded to tell me that now she is being confronted with the fact that he and his current wife have chosen to attend the same church as she.

She enlightened me with the details and the major point for her repeating these facts. That point being, the Lord had spoken to her heart that she needed to forgive him, accept him into the same body of believers, and that they could indeed Glorify God during the same Sunday service.

As she was narrating this set of circumstances, I looked up and there being seated by a hostess was my most despicable Captain. His face fell right in line with the word forgive. Every fiber in my being wanted to shout NO, NO, NO. As she continued to convey the remaining details of her account, my mind could only hear the voice of the Lord telling me "Forgiveness is not given in response to anyone's goodness. Forgiveness is given from a heart of mercy and grace."

Tears started to stain my face. Pitiful site when your mascara runs in the restaurant. My friend, thinking that I am responding to her tale, says, "It's OK, I have since dealt with the situation and my ex-husband is welcome to come to my church."

I respond with how strong and merciful she is to be able to so easily yield to the Lords will. Without hesitation, she tells me that it has not been easy, quite the contrary but shares the joy she has received from knowing that God is pleased with her acceptance.

The following morning, I went to roll call, hit the street, and waited until the Command people started filing into their offices. I came into the station at approximately 9 AM.

I informed my immediate Christian Commander that I would be out of service for a short period of time and explained why. My feelings for this man were no secret to anyone that I worked with. My Commands attitude was one of acceptance and he said that he would pray for me while I was being obedient.

I marched into the "favorite Captain's" office. I asked his Secretary if she would announce my presence and request a moment of his time. The next thing you know, I am sitting across the desk from this man praying that I not back down.

I started off. "Twenty-three years ago, we came on the police department in the same recruitment class. In the years that followed, I have savored, stored and harbored bitterness and much resentment toward you. I don't want to discuss specific situations, nor even mention events that may have precipitated the onslaught of those feelings. I only want to tell you that God has made it very clear that my attitude toward you stands in my way of His forgiving me of my transgressions. Thus I would like to apologize for years of angry thoughts, nasty looks and ask that you forgive me."

He looked at me in complete bewilderment and said, "I can't imagine what you might have been offended by. I would appreciate if you could give me an example."

I, remaining composed, said, "No, we are not going there as that would only reestablish feelings that I have renounced. I ask only that you forgive me and we go forward from here."

He replied, "OK then."

I, then surprising myself, said, "The only other thing is that I would like a hug." I didn't give him a chance to respond but simply walked around his desk and hugged him. I left his office saying, "See you in the halls."

What a rush!! Knowing that you have been obedient to God is the absolute highest high in the world. Crack, cocaine and all the other drugs in the world cannot equal the joy that He gives.

God has a plan. Sometimes it takes years for the realization of that plan while He waits for our steps to catch up to His.

TWENTY-SIX

Leaving My Friends

John 15:4—Remain in me, and I will remain in you. No branch can bear fruit by itself; it must remain in the vine. Neither can you bear fruit unless you remain in me. (NIV)

Twenty-five years is a long period of time. I had a rewarding career, in spite of all the brick walls. Both those imposed upon me, and those I built myself. Recollections, both good and bad, are everlasting. They can be suppressed or they can be savored. I can honestly say that the majority of my law enforcement memories are those that I enjoy reminiscing. The happenings that bring unfavorable emotional responses are placed in the recycling bin to be deleted completely.

Friends are our reward for the nurturing efforts that we afford to one another. One-way friendships don't exist. The definition of friendship requires two or more people to be involved. I will be forever grateful for the relationships that were woven among officers, management, city officials, and the citizens of our great city.

As my days were winding down two of my most treasured friends on the dayshift nominated me for a "Woman of Excellence" award. There were six categories in which women were nominated. The class they chose was "Women Taking Risks."

See Page 124

I was unaware of this until briefly before the award banquet. My family and friends attended. I initially felt infinitely unworthy. Later, as the Lord dealt with my heart, I realized that I represented many other women who were riding in squad cars, answering calls, making judgments without all the necessary information, balancing attitudes of our own with those that are expected of us. I proudly accepted this honor not simply for myself, but for those that follow after me. I pray that God guides and directs their paths.

Everyone knows that women are more emotional than men. I relished my retirement on one hand, and on the other, I missed the daily camaraderie.

After several months, I realized that my ministry had been comprised of the people that I came in contact with through my employment. Never before had I consciously thought about it. I felt an enormous loss. How in the world was I to serve the Lord now?

Duh!! I could start at home. My husband and I, although on the same department had very little time together. We worked different divisions, different hours and seldom had the same days off. This led to 'not knowing each other very well'. We attended church together, lived in the same house, had some friends in common and went on vacations together. Outside of that, I soon realized that we came and went in different directions.

I would love to say that reconnecting was a spontaneous, joyful, exuberant event. It was none of the above. It was filled with expectancies that didn't occur – on both our parts. I found that I had been cooking him meals that he despised. He found that all of a sudden I was more than willing to express my likes and dislikes. We have succeeded in discovering how and why we molded our relationship in the very beginning.

Thank God for Mercy, Truth and Grace.

To the Men and Women of every law enforcement agency, I vow to continue to pray that God go with you not just daily but minute by minute. I pray that you give Him the opportunity to reign in your lives. I pray that you invite him to ride shotgun in your squad car and protect you from harm.

God has a plan and His plans produce.

ABOUT THE AUTHOR

Janell Armstrong believes she was born at exactly the right time and in the right place – at home in a small house in Nebraska. Though she didn't think so at the time, growing up on a working farm was the perfect place for her. Her education consisted of country school, two years of Catholic grade school, four years of Catholic high school, one year of nurse's training, business college and then the police academy. She wanted to do one of everything, and she's still working on it. She hopes you enjoy this book, a small segment of her law enforcement experience.

41182038R00146

Made in the USA
Lexington, KY
02 May 2015